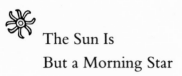 The Sun Is
But a Morning Star

The Sun Is But a Morning Star

Studies in
West Coast Poetry
and Poetics

Lee Bartlett

University of New Mexico Press

ALBUQUERQUE

Library of Congress Cataloging-in-Publication Data

Bartlett, Lee, 1950–
    The sun is but a morning star: studies in West Coast poetry
and poetics / Lee Bartlett.
        p.   cm.
    Bibliography: p.

    ISBN 0-8263-0911-9
    1. American poetry—Pacific Coast (U.S.)—History and
criticism. 2. American poetry—California—San Francisco—
History and criticism. 3. American poetry—20th century—
History and criticism. 4. Pacific Coast (U.S.)—Intellectual
life. 5. San Francisco (Calif.)—Intellectual life. 6. Poetics.
I. Title.
PS281.B37 1989
811'.5409979—dc20   89-9174

Contents

The moon rises late over Mt. Diablo,
Huge, gibbous, warm; the wind goes out,
Brown fog spreads over the bay from the marshes,
And overhead the cry of birds is suddenly
Loud, wiry, and tremulous.

—*Kenneth Rexroth*

Preface

This collection gathers studies on a few West Coast poets who have come into prominence since 1940. It certainly offers no rigorous thematic continuity but rather draws together short pieces (many written for specific occasions) arising out of my continuing interest in a rich body of postmodern American poetry too often undervalued by critics and reviewers. Most of these studies focus on the work of writers specifically identified with the San Francisco Renaissance, in one or another of its incarnations—Kenneth Rexroth, William Everson, Robert Duncan, Gary Snyder, and Michael McClure. I hope that, taken together, they outline a few major projects and themes. The essay on Thom Gunn and Nathaniel Tarn attempts to examine both why these two emigré writers have been attracted to the western ethos and what effect that attraction has had on their work, while the notes on Language poets offer a primer to the work and theoretical concerns of a number of younger poets (especially Michael Palmer and Ron Silliman) often identified with the San Francisco Bay area. A concluding conversation with William Everson and Nathaniel Tarn focuses on such issues as poetic language, the vocation of the poet, and the relationship of West Coast poetry to the larger American landscape.

It is appropriate that the collection open with an essay on Kenneth Rexroth, who served as a presiding figure in the West Coast literary scene from the forties until his death in 1982. He shared a number of the interests of most of the other writers represented here: like William Everson and Gary Snyder his work passionately and accurately evoked the physical geography of the West; like Snyder and Nathaniel Tarn he was continually drawn to poetic sources outside the conventional North American line (like Snyder in particular he found much in Japanese and Chinese poetries), and like them both devoted energy to translation; like most of these poets he sought a poetry of direct communication and sacramental community.

On a more practical level, he aided many of these writers in publication, in particular recommending them to James Laughlin. While most major publishing houses have shown little, if any, interest in West Coast poets in any sustained way, Laughlin's New Directions has of course been the exception, publishing not only Rexroth himself, Everson, Duncan, McClure, Tarn, and a selection of Language poetry, but in either books or the annual New Directions anthologies Kenneth Patchen, Philip Lamantia, Mary Fabilli, George Leite, and many other West Coast writers as well. According to Laughlin, Rexroth "did what Pound had done, giving me books to read and explaining what was good about them. . . . When I could, I'd take his advice about contemporary poets. He put me on to Gary Snyder, William Everson, and a half dozen other fine poets. It was through Kenneth that I learned of Denise Levertov. His taste was excellent." Further, Rexroth edited the seminal second issue of the *Evergreen Review,* "The San Francisco Scene," which in 1957 focused important attention on Everson (as Antoninus), Duncan, Snyder, Michael McClure, and Lawrence Ferlinghetti, as well as Allen Ginsberg and Jack Kerouac. Obviously, without Rexroth's aid much of the work discussed here might well have been completely relegated to the lively but ephemeral world of the small press.

The other primary presence here is William Everson, who for eighteen and a half years was a member of the Dominican order, writing under the name Brother Antoninus. Rexroth offered great support for Everson's work at a crucial point in his career, and through most of their adult lives the two poets were very close. Of Rexroth, Everson wrote, "He touched the nerve of the future and more than any other voice in the movement called it into being"; for his part, Rexroth regarded Everson as "probably the most profoundly moving and durable of the poets of the San Francisco Renaissance . . . the finest Catholic poet writing today." I suppose the source of my interest in Everson's work, and to an extent the work of most of these writers, is that like him I was born in northern California; his landscape is my own in a way that, say, Olson's Gloucester or Lowell's Boston is not. Further, I was raised a Catholic and continue to find the poetry of Everson's Catholic period— which I consider his best—to be the most powerful achievement of any religious writer since the war, certainly ranking with Eliot's later work. Everson's own studies in depth psychology have led me to an appreciation of "the truth and life" of C. G. Jung's myth, and, importantly, the possibility of its reconciliation with Catholic tradition.

Interestingly, while again these writers form no coherent school—representing in fact three generations of West Coast poetry—there are numerous other connections among them. As I've mentioned, Rexroth actively supported the work of Everson, Duncan (though their relationship was problematic), Snyder, McClure, and Tarn, culminating in each publishing with New Directions through his efforts. Robert Duncan's mythopoeic imagination and, in particular, his sense of the poet's vocation fueled a close and lifelong friendship with Everson. Further, both Michael McClure and Thom Gunn have written eloquently of the importance of Duncan's example, while later in his life Duncan offered close friendship and support to Michael Palmer. Gary Snyder, of course, shares Everson's and Tarn's sense of the importance of place, as well as Tarn's particular interest in what has come to be called ethnopoetics. Additionally, like both Rexroth and Tarn, Snyder has found much value in Buddhist traditions. Though neither Rexroth nor Duncan seemed to have much use for many of the so-called Language poets, certainly both shared their interest in linguistic play and, more important, along with Snyder and McClure the insistence of writers like Ron Silliman on the possibility of poetry as a politically transformative force.

While the work of postwar West Coast poets has a wide readership both in this country and abroad, the critical response to this body of poetry over the years has been generally disappointing. As of this writing, the place in the canon occupied by figures like Rexroth, Everson, and Duncan (as well as other writers not discussed here, like Kenneth Patchen, Jack Spicer, and even Robinson Jeffers) remains extremely problematic. When Gary Snyder won the Pulitzer Prize for poetry in 1975 for *Turtle Island,* he became the first California poet, for example, ever to win that award. Jeffers did not, nor has Everson, nor did either Duncan or Rexroth. There is a complex of extraesthetic reasons for this, and the shame is not limited to the exclusion of writers in the West; William Carlos Williams won his only Pulitzer Prize after his death. If, as W. H. Auden said, "prizes are for boys," maybe this fact is unimportant. However, winning major literary awards does much to increase a poet's visibility and certainly adds to his or her attractiveness to critics and anthologists. In his essay, "At the Death of Kenneth Rexroth," Eliot Weinberger's account is emblematic: "I was assigned, at my suggestion, to write an obituary on Kenneth Rexroth for *The Nation,* a magazine he had served for fifteen years as San Francisco correspondent. Written in the week after his death, the article was promptly rejected for 'overpraising a minor writer' (and a 'sexist pig' to boot)." The obituary finally appeared in *Sulfur,* "and only there, in the obscure, sometimes honorable domain of the little magazine, could a condensed version of my small notice of Rexroth's death finally see print."

Rarely has a mainstream critic recognized the achievement of any of these poets. In his recent *A History of Modern Poetry,* for example, David Perkins devotes a few pages to "Minor Poets of San Francisco" (and a few more to Duncan and Snyder), while writers like Robert Lowell and James Merrill occupy full chapters each. Poems like Rexroth's *The Homestead Called Damascus,* Duncan's *Passages,* Everson's *The Rose of Solitude,* Snyder's *Myths & Texts,* McClure's *Ghost Tantras,* Tarn's *Lyrics for the Bride of God,* or Palmer's *Notes for Echo Lake* would have seemed obvious inclusions in M. L. Rosenthal and Sally M. Gall's massive *The Modern Poetic Sequence: The Genius of Modern Poetry.* Yet none of the work by these writers was chosen for discussion; rather, the contemporary landscape is represented by Robert Lowell, W. D. Snodgrass, John Berryman, Allen Ginsberg, Sylvia Plath, and Anne Sexton. Helen Vendler's recent *The Harvard Book of Contemporary American Poetry* contains selections from Wallace Stevens to Amy Clampitt, but again there is no Rexroth, Duncan, Everson, McClure, Palmer, Silliman. To be fair, Vendler includes a few brief Snyder poems, though arguably they are some of his weakest. And generally speaking the critical response to the more recent work of the Language poets has been either hostile or, more often, simply nonexistent. In his essay "The Age of Criticism," Randall Jar-rell astutely advises, "The best critic who ever lived could not prove that the *Iliad* is better than *Trees;* the critic can only state his belief persuasively, and hope that the reader of the poem will agree." I have no interest in these studies in proving that the work of Rexroth is somehow more valuable than Lowell's, that Duncan, Everson, Snyder, Tarn, and Palmer speak to us more adequately than Berryman, Merrill, Snodgrass, or Sexton (though on most days I believe it). Rather, I have simply tried to offer a few ways into some of the work of a number of poets usually identified with the West Coast who have greatly added to the measure of contemporary American poetry.

The older studies of Rexroth, Everson, and Gunn and Tarn are fairly traditional essays looking at a few central aspects of the work and thought of those poets. The more recent pieces on such innovative poets as Duncan, McClure, and Palmer and the Language group, however, are an attempt at a more open, more inclusive approach. They are more than notebook entries— each attempts to make, I hope, a fairly crucial argument. Yet in the manner of collage they do make much use of quotation and secondary sources, and are perhaps more provisional and more personal than the standard critical essay. To an extent I take Duncan's own *H.D. Book* and the more recent work of Sherman Paul as models, as the individual sections are meant to be both generative and reflective.

I should also mention that save for brief discussion in the chapter on Language poets, there are no women poets repre-sented in this collection, a situation I find troubling. However, for reasons which remain to a great extent a mystery to me, until recently women poets on the West Coast (writers like Josephine Miles and Carolyn Kizer) have had nowhere near the measure of influence as their eastern contemporaries. Fortu-nately, though, such younger writers as Leslie Scalapino, Lyn

Hejinian, and Kathleen Fraser, among many others, are power-fully staking their claims to our best attention.

Many of these studies were undertaken for specific occasions: "The Community of Love: Reading Kenneth Rexroth's Long Poems" and "The Theory of the Flower" were originally deliv-ered as lectures; the first subsequently appeared in *The Centen-nial Review,* the second in a substantially different form in *Criti-cal Inquiry.* "God's Crooked Lines: William Everson and C. G. Jung" served as an introduction to a small-press edition of William Everson's *On Writing the Waterbirds.* "Gary Snyder's Han-shan and the Question of Translation" originally appeared in an earlier version in *Sagetrieb,* while "*Myths & Texts* and the Monomyth" was published in *Western American Literature.* Wil-liam Everson's comments on Robert Duncan first appeared in the special Duncan issue of *American Poetry.* Thanks to the editors of those journals—Linda Wagner-Martin, W. J. T. Mit-chell, Burton Hatlen, C. T. Terrell, Thomas J. Lyon—as well as to Beth Hadas and Dana Asbury of the University of New Mexico Press, for their patience and care. Further, the ongoing support of Hamlin Hill, Hobson Wildenthal, F. Chris Garcia, and Paul Risser made the writing of these essays possible.

1 🎲 A Community of Love: Reading Kenneth Rexroth's Long Poems

In his introduction to a *festschrift* for Kenneth Rexroth, Geoffrey Gardner observes that "one of the great paradoxes of Rexroth's enormously paradoxical career is that his widest reputation is for being the promoter of some vaguely defined avant garde of which he is also a member." This is both true and unfortunate: It is true because Rexroth did much to aid younger writers through the years. He was a presiding figure over at least two important "movements" in contemporary writing—the first San Francisco Renaissance of the forties, which brought attention to writers like Robert Duncan, William Everson, Philip Lamantia, and Thomas Parkinson, and the later Beat Generation, which proved a breakthrough for Allen Ginsberg, Gary Snyder, Michael McClure, Diane DiPrima, Philip Whalen, and others. It is unfortunate because Rexroth's efforts in this area, and his finely honed polemical skill which he put at the service of those writers and causes he believed in, have tended to overshadow (and he is not unlike Ezra Pound in this regard) his achievement as a poet.

Writing an assessment a few months after the poet's death in the summer of 1982, Eliot Weinberger argued that "Rexroth at his death was among the best known and least read of American poets. It is a sad distinction he shares, not coincidentally, with the poet he most resembles, Hugh MacDiarmid. . . . Nevertheless, there is no question that American literary history will have to be rewritten to accommodate Rexroth, that postwar American poetry is the 'Rexroth Era' as much (and as little) as the earlier decades are the 'Pound Era.' "[1]

Certainly, the critical response to Rexroth's poetry has been disappointing, though from the start by defining himself as antiacademic and small and alternative-press oriented, Rexroth himself is at least in part responsible for the academy's deaf ear. In his introduction to D. H. Lawrence's *Selected Poems* (published by New Directions in 1947), for example, Rexroth threw down the gauntlet before the New Critics. "Any bright young man can be taught to be artful," he wrote. "It is always the lesser artists who are artful, they must learn their trade by rote." And again, "I suppose it is the absolutism which has encouraged the ignorant to expect a canzone of Dante's in each issue of their favorite little magazine, a School of Athens in every WPA mural." And the final blast, "Men and women torture each other to death in the bedroom, just as the dying dinosaurs gnawed each other as they copulated in the chilly marshes. . . . When we show signs of waking, another cocktail instead of the Wine of God."[2] In a period in America when Lawrence's reputation was less than flourishing and when poetry was progressively being taken over by university writers and critics who had cut their teeth on Brooks and Warren's *Understanding Poetry,* such a salvo was a kind of declaration of war on the literary status quo.

Rexroth's long-standing feud with Leslie Fiedler was emblematic. In 1948, Fiedler reviewed William Everson's *Residual Years* for the *Partisan Review,* a book gathering much of Everson's antiwar poetry which Rexroth convinced James Laughlin to publish and for which he wrote the jacket copy. Fiedler didn't review the poetry per se at all; rather he focused his attack on the blurb. "The jacket blurb is a kind of manifesto: poems are to be no longer 'abstract aesthetic objects,'" he began, "but intimate speech, sensuous and passionate. The paired adjectives suggest, of course, Milton, but is D. H. Lawrence via Rexroth and Patchen, who is actually invoked, and we should perhaps read for the more conventional pair—phallic and sentimental. . . . For Everson, Lawrence serves primarily as a guarantor for the transference of bad writing, that is to say, flagrant sentimentalizing about, copulation from prose to what is, presumably, verse."[3] Through the fifties Rexroth and Fiedler would periodically take potshots at each other, culminating in Rexroth's 1968 review for the *New York Times Book Review,* "Leslie Fiedler: Custer's Last Stand." There, Rexroth would write:

> Fiedler is possessed by a number of obsessions
> which destroy his convincingness, except amongst
> people who don't know better. First, as is well
> known, is his favorite term of abuse, "WASP." He
> uses it the way Stalinists used to write "Trotskyite,"
> for the most incongruous assortment of writers and
> tendencies. Since he sees White Anglo-Saxon Prot-
> estants under every bed and in every woodpile, it is
> easy for him to identify the main line of American
> culture with their works and to prove that this cul-
> ture has been continuously challenged and is now
> collapsing from within. Ultimately this is an incur-
> able distortion of vision due to membership in a
> small circle of extremely ethnocentric people—the
> self-styled New York Establishment, triangulated by
> the *Partisan Review, The New York Review of Books,*
> and *Commentary.* The United States is a big country,
> and this tiny set is not even an epi-center, but a
> small disturbance on an epicycle.[4]

To a certain extent Fiedler was right in his assessment of Rexroth's aesthetic as "sentimental," in that for the most part Rexroth represented an American revival of a kind of neoromanticism over against the prevailing neoclassic formalism represented, for example, by the early Robert Lowell. In England, such a revival had begun with poets like Dylan Thomas and David Gascoyne and was now embodied in the writers of the "New Apocalypse," figures like Henry Treece, J. P. Hendry, Alex Comfort, and Vernon Watkins. In his "Unacknowledged Legislators and Art Pour Art," first given as a lecture at the University of Southern California Library in 1958, Rexroth provided a loosely argued manifesto, one to which a number of other neoromantic West Coast poets like William Everson and Gary Snyder would subscribe. The lecture is a brief and casual examination of the nature of poetry: "I think the best way to start is naively and empirically to say that poetry is what poets write and poets are what the public generally agrees are poets." One of poetry's qualities, as in the work of Catullus, is the communication of "the most intense experiences of very developed sensibilities," and this communication is open to anyone who is receptive, regardless of the poet's envisioned audience. As the poem exists through time, "it performs historically and socially the function of symbolic criticism of values" through the organization "of sensibility so that it is not wasted. Thus, we became more clearly aware of what is good and bad, interesting and dull, beautiful and ugly, loveable and mean."

Over against the new critical assessment of the art object as primarily acontextual, for Rexroth communication is the key; the only difference between poetry and domestic speech, he continues, is that poetry "communicates more; in fact, the epistemological dilemmas of modern thought have never existed for anybody except Western man. . . . The epistemological problems arose as in Europe and America human relationships became increasingly abstract," a problem more recently taken up by writers like Michael Palmer and Ron Silliman, "and the relation of men to their work became more remote. Six men who have worked together to build a boat or a house with their own hands do not doubt of its existence." The poet certainly has a political responsibility, but the communication poets offer which remains of interest is not programmatic, and often "consciously tendentious poets are crippled by their 'message.'" Art does not hold out for us some kind of imagined historical progress; rather, if anything changes over time, it is an ever-widening "sensibility." If there is any kind of progress in the arts, Rexroth concludes it is "the progress in their means, in their instruments and in a slow growth towards more widespread purity."[5]

Throughout his myriad essays and reviews, Rexroth offers a kind of guide to those writers, artists, and thinkers who achieve this deepened sensibility: the visionary painter Morris Graves, Baudelaire and Celine (both of whom "face the monster all the time"), Martin Buber, Mark Tobey, Lawrence Durrell, Denise Levertov, Balzac, Samuel Beckett (who is "so great because he has said the final word to date in the long indictment of industrial and commercial civilization which began with Blake and Sade"), and many others. He finds the "long-term" tendencies of modern American verse in particular to "reflect the major influences that went to form the culture as a whole and these in turn the ethnic and national groups who have made up the American people." He has special praise for Yvor Winters, Raymond Larson, Jean Toomer, Kenneth Patchen, and again Denise Levertov. Pound, Eliot, and Stevens receive mixed evaluations. He takes issue with Charles Olson ("there is nothing here that is not in H.D. . . . Olson turns out to have had a heavy and conventional ear"), as well as Hart Crane, Richard Wilbur, and Allen Tate. He calls William Carlos Williams "the greatest prosodist of his generation because he is its greatest poet."

James Wright has written that Rexroth "is a great love poet during the most loveless of times," and indeed over the past sixty years Rexroth has written some of the most moving and durable American verse of our century. Undoubtedly, Rexroth's most well-known and accessible poems are his lyrics and his translations. Additionally, however, he wrote five long "philosophical" poems; these comprise his 1968 volume, *The Collected Longer Poems*. The first of these, *The Homestead Called Damascus*, was written while he was still in his teens; the last, *Heart's Garden, The Garden's Heart*, was not completed until after the collection itself had gone to New Directions. In between we have *A Prolegomenon to a Theodicy, The Phoenix and the Tortoise*, and *The Dragon and the Unicorn*. Interestingly, while criticism of the last decade has found the modern long poem a fruitful area of inquiry (I'm thinking here of fine studies like M. L. Rosenthal and Sally M. Gall's *The Modern Poetic Sequence*, Barry Ahern's study of *Zukofsky's "A"*, and countless books and articles on *The Cantos, Paterson, The Maximus Poems, Life Studies*, and *The Dream Songs*), Rexroth's long poems have received very little attention. Yet it seems to me that taken together these five poems form as interesting and coherent a major poetic project as any of the other great long poems of this century, and certainly if Rexroth's work survives it will be in large measure because of his achievement here. At the very least, his long poem offers an alternative vision and set of stylistic possibilities to what was the prevailing formalist aesthetic.

In his introduction to *The Collected Longer Poems*, Rexroth explains that he considers these poems as sections of a larger single project, rather than as discreet entities: "All the sections of this book now seem to me almost as much one long poem as do the *The Cantos* or *Paterson*. . . . The plot remains the same—

the interior and exterior adventures of two poles of personality." Further, he notes that "the political stance of the poems never changes: the only Absolute is the Community of Love with which Time ends. . . . I have tried to embody in verse the belief that the only valid conservation of value lies in the assumption of unlimited liability, the supernatural identification of the self with the tragic unity of the creative process."[6] Though it is doubtful that Rexroth wrote *The Homestead Called Damascus,* at least, with either Pound's or Williams's notion of a grand modern epic in progress, I would like to look at the poem in some detail because it establishes the twin geometries explored by the poet in his later longer work, and is probably the least well known of the long poems.

The publication history of *Homestead* is a little tangled. Rexroth began the poem when he was just fifteen and completed it not later than 1925, at age twenty. Two sections ("Adonis in Summer" and "Adonis in Winter") from Part II appeared as short poems in *The Phoenix and the Tortoise* (1944), but the poem entire was not published until 1957 in *The Quarterly Review of Literature* (where it was followed by a series of notes by Lawrence Lipton, and won a Longview Award). New Directions finally released the poem as a separate volume in its "World Poets" pamphlet series in 1963.

Homestead is juvenilia, but (like "the Lovesong of J. Alfred Prufrock," completed when Eliot was just twenty-three) it is certainly not slight. "In those days," Rexroth wrote Lawrence Lipton, "we thought *The Wasteland* a revolutionary poem,"[7] and while commentators have seen the influence of both Aiken and Jeffers in *Homestead,* it is obvious that the poem is Rexroth's youthful attempt to meet Eliot's challenge. Like *The Wasteland, Homestead* is divided into sections, its intelligibility depends upon both a literate audience and readers willing to work through a rather discontinuous narrative structure, and throughout we sense that no less than the very core of Western Civilization is at stake. Even the language of the poem recalls Eliot's early work.

> And Thomas, with a narrow light,
> Comes out and watches, by the gate;
> And muses in the turgid night;
> And goes into the house again.
> The library is calm and prim.
> The shepherds and the sheep have passed.
> And Botticelli ladies, slim
> And hyperthyroid, grace the walls

However, while Eliot's allusiveness seems somehow fully integrated into his long poem, Rexroth's often does not. "I was immersed in Frazier, Murray, Harrison, Jessie Weston, A. E. Waite, and was busy reading the whole corpus of the Arthuriad" (42), the poet noted to Lipton, and many times here Rexroth seems to be wearing his learning on his sleeve, as his frequent literary, philosophical, and historical allusions are sometimes merely gratuitous. Still, I think that because of its structural complexity, the loveliness of certain passages, and the fact that the poem announces themes that will play throughout the other, more mature longer poems, *Homestead* remains an integral part of Rexroth's corpus. And as the product of a teenage mind, it is remarkable.

The poem is divided into four numbered sections, with the fourth section divided into two parts. Lipton has noted that the "mood" of the work is that of elegiac reverie, though this reverie alternates with straight narrative passages. There are three narrative consciousnesses here—Thomas Damascan, his brother Sebastian, and a disembodied narrative voice who in his comments on the action seems (as Morgan Gibson points out)[8] as dispassionate and omniscient as Eliot's Tiresias. Rexroth has spoken of these three voices as components of a single personality, his own. Flatly stated, the plot of the poem follows the general pattern of a quest tale. It begins with a twenty-two-line meditation by, presumably, the third narrative voice, which contrasts unquestioning angels ("robed/in tubular, neuter folds of pink and blue") with searching young minds ("poking in odd / Corners for unsampled vocations / Of the spirit, / While the flesh is strong"). Following, we discover that two brothers, Thomas and Sebastian (and the religious implications here are, of course, deliberate), lead rather idyllic lives on the family estate in the Catskills—hiking, reading books like *The Golden Bough,* and sitting up late "drinking wine, / Playing chess, arguing—Plato and Leibnitz, Einstein, Freud and Marx." This pastoral scene ("The sheep are passing in the snow") alternates with the thoroughly modern ("The dim lit station, the late slow train, / And the city of steel and concrete towers") as the boys contemplate the possibility of love as a stay against mortality. The section ends on a harsh note as Sebastian sets the possibility of happiness with his female neighbor Leslie against a sense of the inevitability of death, while Thomas weighs the memory of "panthers' soft cries" in their mating against "Death / Here hinges fall, a land of crusts and / Rusted keys . . . Hakeldama, the potters' field / Full of dead strangers."

In Part II, Thomas crosses the mountains for the "empty city from which / Alternate noise and utter stillness" come, leaving Sebastian to make his way back home alone through the "vegetable light." Sebastian sits playing chess by himself now, drinking "bitter tea," dwelling on his loneliness. In the "deep blue winter evening" he recalls an earlier trip of his own to New York City, remembering dirty snow, pigeons, burnt fried potatoes, a streetcar, and, most vividly, a stripper who "rolls her buttocks" while "rhinestones cover her bee-stung / Pussy and perch on each nipple." But this reverie only intensifies his feeling of separation "through the level days," and his preoccupation with death. It is Good Friday, and Thomas reenters the poem involved (like Tammuz, the slain harvest god) in some sort of "involuntary" sacrifice, the martyrdom Sebastian fears. "How short a time for a life to last," the third voice muses, "So few years, so narrow a space, so / Slight a melody, a handful of / Notes."

Part III is subtitled "The Double Hellas," and here we have sexuality split into its two guises—the erotic and the domestic. We get a sense of the inexorable process of time as the section opens with a description of the earth's movement into and out of the Ice Age. Following, there is a description of the brothers' early pastoral life ("The yellow lights, the humming tile stove, / Father with his silver flute, / Mother singing to the harmonium") but, as Gibson suggests, this environment embodies the "bourgeois-Christian-Classical tradition" which is now, for them both, merely an "ornate, wasted fiction" (36). The erotic is introduced as Sebastian strolls through the garden while "The floral vulvas of orange and crimson / Squirm inside his head." There are allusions to Kore (Persephone, whose yearly return to the world from Hades symbolized fecundity), Chlorus (beautiful wife to King Neleus), "Pisanello's courtesans," and Maxine (the black stripper from Part II), but these only confuse Sebastian further. In the modern world there seems to be no room for passion, no room for the heroic: "the epic hero / Came, in full armour, making a huge / Clatter, and fell, struck down from behind / . . . the clock ticks measured out his death." As Maxine sleeps in her far-off "scented bed," Sebastian reads Socrates on love in solitude. "Shall personal / Loneliness give way to the enduring / Geological isolation?" he wonders. Meanwhile, Thomas comments on the nature of the family estate, "a land too well-mannered" where "the bedrooms / Mold with the sweat of bygone death beds." Unlike Sebastian, he has a distinct lack of interest in domestic sexuality: "Her thighs, her buttocks rolling like two / Struggling slugs—these things are not for me," for the "echoing in the tunneled / Sepulcher" presages death.

What follows is a meditation on presence by the third narrative voice. The beautiful world of the thing—a new brick warehouse, lovers, cattle—is for Thomas his "sacrament," an "undeniable reality": "Heraclitus said that the world was made / Of the quick red tongue between her lips, / Or else from the honey that welled up / From the shady spring between the thighs." But again, like "the tree, moon isolate / In a moonless night, stiffens in an / Explosion of wind and rips off every / Leaf," the human world is ever-winding down, ever deteriorating, "Dun camels in the smoky desert, / The Pyramids gone crimson into time." All that is left us is "music of objects worn by careful hands."

The final section of *Homestead*, "The Stigmata of Fact," continues with images of death and deterioration: "chalk old skulls," "a crumbling kingdom," "assassins everywhere," "the thick dust / Settles once more on the disordered / Bones in their endless sleep." Such is Thomas's "brilliant / Summer region, his painted landscape." For a time, Sebastian is able to make a leap of faith ("I am the Master of the / Pattern of my life") which leads him momentarily to his dying mother and Maxine. In the end, though, he finds himself a kind of Prufrock, "Dead? / No, living with a limitless sterile / Kind of life . . . naked, / Blind, salty, and relaxed on the edge / Of the blind sea alone with the blind rabbi." The great myths—Theseus, the Minotaur, the labyrinth—and the Easter Island statues have been reduced to dust by modern archeology. Leaving Sebastian, "puzzled" in the rain-soaked slums, Thomas retreats to the mountains, the lights of the modern city disappearing behind the "tiny, closing doors of silence."

In *Homestead*, then, we have a number of themes to which

Rexroth will return again and again. The brothers are a kind of split consciousness—the active (Sebastian) over against the reflective (Thomas); or, as Gibson prefers, "the tendency toward sacrifice and martyrdom, and the restraining tendency of skeptical withdrawal from commitment" (41)—a split the poet will struggle with in himself throughout his life. There is the romantic's despair over the passing of both the mythic imagination and the natural world, along with an intense sense of *carpe diem*. And perhaps most important, there is a seeking after the fact of heterosexual love, which in the contemporary world has seemingly lost not only its sacramental nature but its significance as a transformative power as well. Unlike Matthew Arnold's Dover Beach lovers, Thomas is left not with the grail but squatting in the darkness at a fire, alone.

Rexroth began *A Prolegomenon to a Theodicy* in 1925 and finished it two years later; this poem didn't appear until 1949, however, when it was included in *The Art of Worldly Wisdom*, and it has never been published separately. While *Homestead* is in large part meditative, *A Prolegomenon* is more experimental; in fact the severe dissociation and juxtaposition are reminiscent of Cubist painting, an interest of Rexroth's at the period.

Though the case might be made that here Rexroth was primarily concerned with stylistic possibilities, the poem's primary argument continues the movement of *Homestead*. A prolegomenon is a preface, an introduction; a theodicy is the concept of the vindication of the goodness of God in respect to the existence of evil. If God is supremely good and supremely powerful, goes the age-old Christian paradox, and if he cannot make an error, how is it that evil can exist in the world? The poem continues the despair of *Homestead* in its opening section: "I want something else / I want and want always wear and wear / Always / Always / But you can't have it don't you realize there / Isn't any more there isn't any more at all not / At all"

(43). The next many sections provide catalogues of objects, actions, concepts seen through the "anagogic eye," as Rexroth moves for resolution, not through logic but after "the visionary experience without which no theodicy is possible" (45). By the poem's conclusion, its Christian imagery emerges fully developed ("The bread of light / The chalice of the abyss / The wine of flaming light"), as the poet has moved through a kind of apocalypse to the appearance of God. To my mind, this odd poem offers no satisfactory solution to its own paradox, save a kind of willed acceptance. Certainly its primary question continues Rexroth's search for some kind of transcendent vision (though interestingly there is little reference to the power of physical love here), but finally it seems a mere exercise.

With *The Phoenix and the Tortoise* (the title poem of his second book, published in 1944), Rexroth has settled into his more mature style. Here he engages more directly the question of "the Community of Love" he spoke about in the introduction to *The Homestead* and the Cubist experiment of *Prolegomenon* offering the more direct, personal statement we have come to associate with Rexroth's mature work (as well as that of western poets for whom he has been a direct influence, like Gary Snyder and William Everson). Further, the poet's political engagement becomes an important element in this poem, and it is the first of his long poems which is set, at least in part, in California.

The entire collection (the volume also contains a number of shorter lyrics, as well as translations and "imitations") attempts to develop, Rexroth tells us in his introductory note, "more or less systematically, a definite point of view . . . the discovery of a basis for the recreation of a system of values in sacramental marriage." *Phoenix* attempts "to portray the whole process" ("from abandon to erotic mysticism, from erotic mysticism to the ethical mysticism of sacramental marriage, thence to the realization of the ethical mysticism of universal responsibility") in "historical, personal, and physical terms." He dedicates the poem to Albert Schweitzer, "the man," he says, "who, in our time, pre-eminently has realized the dream of Leonardo da Vinci."

Like the first long poem, we have again a quest of sorts, as *Phoenix* opens with the poet meditating on "the geological past / Of the California Coast Ranges," figures of death along the coast:

> Of what survives and what perished,
> And how, of the fall of history
> And waste of fact—on the crumbling
> Edge of a ruined polity
> That washes away in an ocean
> Whose shores are all washing into death.
>
> A group of terrified children
> Has just discovered the body
> Of a Japanese sailor bumping
> In a snarl of kelp in a tidepool.

The poet is again a seeker, "seeking the continuity, / The germ plasm, of history, / The epic's lyric absolute." What, he asks, is the relationship between art and history? Can anything transcend the ravages of time? History, he tells us, is composed of mere "particulars," while poetry offers "an imaginary / Order of being, where existence / And essence, as in the Diety / Of Aquinas, fuse into pure act." The first section concludes with a privileging of this imaginary order, this mystic vision ("The illimitable hour glass / Of the universe eternally / Turning") over such notions as will and ego.

In the next two sections of the poem, lying under the moonlight in his "folded blanket" next to his wife while "north of us lies the vindictive / Foolish city asleep under its guns," the poet expresses his anarchism: "The State is the organization / Of the evil instincts of mankind"; "War is the State"; "Man is a social animal; / That is, top dog to a slave state." The goal of history "is the achievement / Of the completely atomic / Individual and the pure / Commodity relationship . . . / The flow of interoffice / Memoranda charts the excretions of societal process, / The cast snakeskin, the fleeting / Quantum, Economic Man." This angry meditation on modern life and organizational man rumbles through the night until at dawn the poet wonders "would it have been better to have slept / And dreamed, than to have watched night / Pass and this slow moon sink?" Perhaps his wife's "dreams" hold more of an answer than his own "meditations in cold solitude."

A resolution to death and decay, and to man's own corporate stupidities and inhumanities, is offered in the poem's concluding section, wherein like Voltaire's Candide, Rexroth turns to the garden of the personal:

> Babies are more
> Durable than monuments, the rose
> Outlives Ausonius, Ronsard,
> And Waller, and Horace's pear tree
> His immortal column. Once more
> Process is precipitated
> In the receptive womb.
> In the decay of the sufficient
> Reasonableness of sacraments
> Marriage holds by its bona fides.

Nude, he enters the water, "the prime reality," and it is the sudden appearance of this wife, also naked, which offers a transcendent, even beatific vision, a final alternative to dead men "in the ancient rubbish": "The sun crosses / The hills and fills her hair, as it lights / The moon and glorifies the sea / And deep in the empty mountains melts / The snow of Winter and the glaciers / Of ten thousand years."

The Dragon and the Unicorn (written between 1944 and 1950, and published in 1952) opens where *Phoenix* leaves off. If love is the answer to the paradox of history, just what is its nature? Written in the direct style of the earlier poem, this is by far Rexroth's longest poem (running over 6,000, primarily seven-syllable, lines), and certainly one of his most fully realized. While the setting of *Phoenix* is northern California, *Dragon* follows the poet across America, through Europe, back to San Francisco. As Rexroth notes in his preface to the volume, "The form is that of the travel poems of Samuel Rogers and Arthur Hugh Clough. The general tone is not far removed from that expressed by other American travellers abroad, notably Mark Twain." Yet again the poet is off on a quest, and yet again the quest is bodied forth, as Gibson notes, "as interior monologue of Rexroth's inquiry into the problem of love" (86).

The first of the poem's five parts takes Rexroth (by *Phoenix,* at the very least, the question of an Eliotic persona no longer obtains, the speaker is, clearly, the poet himself) by train from San Francisco to New York, then through the British Isles. Like the previous poem, the political dimension is paramount, as Rexroth again assails the modern city as well as the corporate state. In Chicago, for example, "Man / Gets daily sicker and his / Ugliness knots his bowels. / On the site of several / Historical brothels / Stands the production plant of / Time-Luce Incorporated," In Liverpool, he sees "bombed-out shells, / Everybody too busy / To fix them up. So Rome died." Set against the city, however, he discovers North Wales "glowing with Spring— / Birds and wild flowers everywhere," while

> High above Yarcombe the wind
> Dies at sunset and I rest

In a hanging meadow. The land
Falls away for long blue miles
Down the trough of glacial valley.
In the deep resonant twilight
The stars open like wet flowers.

Yet he returns to London, a place "sicker than New York," as
the answer to his quest is not in the solitude of the pastoral, but
again in a kind of human communion: "There is no reality /
Except that of experience / And experience is the / Conversation of persons." There he searches (often humorously, as with
"Nini," a sadist who "gets quite rough") for love, "the ultimate
/ Mode of free evaluation. / Perfect love casts out knowledge."

At the start of Part II, Rexroth receives copies of *The Art of
Worldly Wisdom* but finds in his new book's pages not the inten-
sity of experience but "only anecdotes for company"; "I cannot
find the past." The setting for this section is France, and the tone
throughout is rather grim, as the poet meditates both on his
own failed attempts at love and the excesses of history. Travel-
ing along the Loire he muses that "Ultimately the fulfillment /
Of reality demands that / Each person in the universe / Realize
every one of the / Others in the fullness of love." Here the
institution of the Church, another manifestation for him of the
corporate state, "is the symbol / Of the repression of all / That I
love in France." Sexual love offers an alternative, but "only for
so brief a time." Rather, it is a deeper, more lastingly transcendent love, a true communion or community, that "like all the
sacraments, is a / Miniature of being itself."

In Part III the scene shifts to Italy, where Rexroth travels
now with his wife, Marthe. Again, he broods on the evils of
collectivity—from capitalism and the Church to the state and
various intellectuals; even social activism is not immune. Echoing Henry Treece's manifesto delineating the New Apocalypse

aesthetic of such younger British poets as Alex Comfort and Vernon Watkins, that "the salvation of the individual man is via the individual man himself and not by way of the Commonwealth, the State, or the International Collective," Rexroth writes:

I know of
No association of men
Which cannot be demonstrated
To have been, ultimately
Organized for purposes
Of coercion and mutual
Destruction. By far the worst
Are the putative communal
And benevolent gangsters. Lawrence pointed out long ago
That the most malignant form
Of hate is benevolence.
Social frightfulness has increased
In exact proportion to
Humanitarianism. . . .
Every collectivity
Is opposed to community.

And again, that community is realized through a sacramental, personal, heterosexual love that in the modern world is constantly in danger of perversion. The only absolute, the only hope of salvation, is the "full communion of lovers," and the section ends in a kind of fulfillment of his vision, with Marthe pregnant.

Part IV takes the poet first to Switzerland. Here he takes issue with Protestantism—"the anal ghost of Karl Barth's church / Of spiritual masochism"—and Jung, then back to Paris and Bordeaux (where he rejects Marxism—"No collectivity against / Collectivities can function / To restore community." Finally, in Part V Rexroth returns to America, and as he travels back across land to San Francisco, he is not pleased: "Calvinist and Liberal / Both strive to reduce moral / Action to the range of the / Objectively guaranteed /. . . . In Kansas even the horses / Look like Landon, ugly parched / Faces like religious turtles." Through capitalism, the East and heartland have become "a ruined country," their inhabitants "a ruining people," though as he moves west out of the morass of the great eastern cities his black mood lifts. Here, out of "the world of purpose," he comes to understand that "the community of persons" transcends even the need for a god. Once again he has returned to the garden of his West to achieve in nature a transcendence of the "empiric ego."

The last of the long poems, *Heart's Garden / The Garden's Heart,* was written over twenty-five years later, in 1967 in Kyoto. The scene is Japan, and once again we have the wandering, meditative, now older poet: "A man of / Sixty years, still wandering / Through wooded hills, gathering / Mushrooms, bracken fiddle necks, / And bamboo shoots, listening / Deep in his mind to music." The mood is Taoist, feminine ("The dark woman is the gate. . . . / She is possessed without effort"), but again he is lost and confused. Pilate's question in *Dragon* appears again, "what is love," but now in his old age Rexroth seems to move beyond argument in favor of, as Gibson argues, complete presentation: "The poem *is* vision; for the sounds and silences of speech unify the poet's sensations. The unity, the harmony, of speech and perception *is* the Tao" (125). The other long poems, even *Dragon,* seem to strain for a vision, as if by enumerating the endless follies of contemporary civilization the poet will finally convince himself (and us) of the necessity of community. Here, however, Rexroth seems no longer to be struggling. The world, like the Tao, simply is, and it is lovely.

In *Homestead,* Rexroth had staked out his twin poles—the life of action (represented by Sebastian) over against the life of reflection (represented by Thomas). By the time of the publication of his collection of shorter poems, *The Signature of All Things,* in 1950, however, he had already come to be drawn more closely to the latter. In that collection, which takes its title from the seventeenth-century mystic Jacob Boehme, he writes in the preface, "Perhaps the integral person is more revolutionary than any program, party, or social conduct." He is coming to accept Boehme's notion of reality, that "the whole outward visible world with all its being is a signature, or figure on the inward spiritual world . . . as the spirit of each creature sets forth and manifests the internal form of its body, so does the Eternal Being also."[9]

I spoke earlier of *Homestead* as, at least in part, the young Rexroth's attempt to meet the challenge of Eliot's *Wasteland;* certainly, *Garden's Heart / The Heart's Garden* in the same fashion works as a counter to Eliot's late great work, *The Four Quartets.* Where Eliot's earlier poem affects impersonal presentation, where it is discontinuous, where it is highly allusive, and where it offers at least in part a social critique, the *Four Quartets* strives for a more personal, discursive voice, is far less allusive, and eschews social critique in favor of what David Perkins calls "Romantic metaphysical exploration."[10] All of this can be said of Rexroth's last long poem as well. However, throughout *The Four Quartets* we have the nagging sense that for all the richness of its imagery and insight, Eliot's vision, tied specifically to an Anglo-Catholic theology in which the Church itself becomes the final point where "the timeless and time intersect," is rather narrowly and exclusively defined. Rexroth's final vision, on the other hand, for all its Asian imagery, is far more Emersonian, far more indigenously American, than Eliot's.

Through the first four long poems the poet's search for a perfect community of love takes him through most pathways of the world's maze, yet none offers an all-encompassing transcendent vision. Here, in his last years, as Eliot embraces the architecture of the Church and its mythologies, for Rexroth politics, literature, sociology all give way to the "music of the waterfall," as he returns to his Penelope, "the final woman who weaves, / And unweaves, and weaves again." And it is this return to nature, quietude, and the feminine which offers the final clarity:

> In the moon-drenched night the floating
> Bridge of dreams breaks off. The clouds
> Banked against the mountain peak
> Dissipate in the clear sky.

"We are unaware that we live in the light of lights," Rexroth closes in his introduction to *The Collected Longer Poems*, "because it casts no shadow. When we become aware of it we know it as birds know air and fish know water. It is the ultimate trust."

2 🌞 God's Crooked Lines:
William Everson and C. G. Jung

Most postmodern poets writing in English probably have been influenced by the general notions of analytical psychology at least to some extent. Reading poem after poem by those writers we associate with a certain primitivism (Ted Hughes, Theodore Roethke, Sylvia Plath, Clayton Eshleman, the list goes on and on), we feel immediately at least the unconscious presence of Jung. Further, some of our most influential recent poets have read rather thoroughly in Jung and have been more directly influenced by his thought. *Spring 1979: An Annual of Archetypal Psychology and Jungian Thought* carries two articles which begin an archeology of Charles Olson's deep interest in analytical psychology. Robert Bly's immersion in Jung's work has taken him into an examination of both the Great Mother and Father archetypes, while Clayton Eshleman's has led him into the caves of the "paleolithic imagination" and to *Sulfur*.[1] Of all postmodern poets of consequence, however, William Everson has probably come closest to being a Jungian disciple, and this vision, this discipline, permeates his work. Here I would like to trace the origins of Everson's interest in analytical psychology, then examine two of the poet's core notions: his view of the poet's vocation as sourced in the prophetic/shamanistic tradi-

23

tion and his stress on the necessity of a recognition of the anima/animus as a prelude to androgyny, a way to God.

In 1932 Jung had written that "among my patients in the second half of life—that is to say, over thirty-five—there has not been one whose problem in the last resort was not that of finding a religious outlook on life."[2] In 1948 Everson was a year beyond Jung's climacteric. He had undergone a series of traumas, including the deaths of both his mother (to whom he was very close) and his father (from whom he was more or less estranged), internment during the war in a camp for conscientious objectors, estrangement and divorce from his first wife Edwa Poulson, and finally a love affair, then second marriage to the poet Mary Fabilli which was on unstable ground, to say the least. In the fall, Fabilli (who at this time was rediscovering her lost Catholic faith) gave Everson a copy of St. Augustine's *Confessions,* wherein he discovered something he "most desperately needed—a man's religion" to replace his rather vaguely defined and failing atheism. On Christmas Eve, Fabilli took Everson to Midnight Mass in a San Francisco cathedral where "the nuns had prepared the Crib to one side of the sanctuary, with fir trees banked about a miniature stable."

> There, suddenly, as he crouched out there on the
> sheepflats of man's terrestial ambiguity, with
> nothing but the rags of pitiful pride between me and
> that death something was spoken into my soul, and
> hearing I followed. When the fir-smelling reached
> me across the closed interior air of the Cathedral,
> binding as it did the best of my past and the best of
> my future, shaping for the first time that synthesis
> of spirit and sense I had needed and never found, I
> was drawn across, and in the smell of the fir I saw it
> for the first time, not merely as an existent thing,

but as a created thing, witness of the Word, the divine Logos, who made all earth, and me, a soul in his own image, out of very love. And I saw in the fact of Creation the end of Creation; and in the end of Creation saw indeed the unspeakable Lover who draws the loved one out of the web of affliction, remakes him as His own. It was then that I could rise from the pew, and following like a hound the trace on the air, go where the little images lay, in the Crib there, so tiny, among the simple beasts, watched over by the cleanly woman and the decent man, and these humble ones, my good friends the sheepherders, who in that instant outleaped the philosophers. That was the night I entered into the family and fellowship of Christ—made my assent, such as it was—one more poor wretch, who had nothing to bring but his iniquities.[3]

Following this experience, Everson took instruction in the Catholic faith, converted, worked for a time with the Catholic Worker Movement in Oakland, California, then eventually entered the Dominican order as Brother Antoninus. Until this time, he had a rising reputation as a poet of the California Central Valley; after a few years of monastic silence, he emerged again on the literary scene replacing in books like *The Crooked Lines of God, The Hazards of Holiness,* and *The Rose of Solitude* his early concerns with man's relationship to the land with man's relationship to God. As Antoninus, Everson became the leading exponent of erotic mysticism in the Church, and with Thomas Merton he enjoyed a reputation as one of the two finest Catholic poets since Gerard Manley Hopkins. This reputation went into slight eclipse when Everson left the order to marry in 1969, but the 1978 publication of his collected Catholic poetry,

The Veritable Years, reawakened critical interest in his achievement. And it is this work from Everson's Catholic period
which is most thoroughly grounded in analytical psychology.

Everson came to Jung through Father Victor White. Fr.
White, like the poet a Dominican, was Reader in Theology at
Blackfriars College at Oxford. Additionally, he was a foundation member and lecturer at the Jung Institute of Analytical
Psychology, and he knew Jung as both a teacher and a friend.
Fr. White visited Jung at Bollengen numerous times and carried
on a substantial correspondence with him which led, unfortunately, to an alienation between the two men late in Jung's life.
For many years Fr. White had planned to write an extended
historical, psychoanalytical, and theological treatise on the relationship between God and the unconscious, but his work was,
he felt, preempted by Albert Beguin's *L'Art romantique et la rêve,*
A. Wilwol's *Ratsel der Seele,* and Josef Goldbrunner's *Heliigkeit
und Gesundheit,* among other books. However, the first two
chapters of this unfinished project, along with ten other related
papers, were collected in 1952 in White's *God and the Unconscious.*

Everson did not read that book until a few years after its
publication, and even then, as he explains in his introduction to
the volume's recent reissue, he was "suspicious of depth psychology's pertinence to the spiritual life, preferring to suffer it
out with St. John of the Cross." Everson met Fr. White in the
fall of 1955, when the priest was a visiting lecturer at St. Albert's College in Oakland, where Everson lived as a lay brother.
There the two men had discussions centering on "the doctrine
of the non-essentiality of evil as seen in the abiding tradition of
the Church since Augustine, which Jung opposed." Eventually,
however, as Everson outlined to me in a letter, Fr. White's work
on Jung took hold of the poet.

Fr. White went back to England after the Spring Se-
mester in 1956. He had been sent Marcuse's *Eros and
Civilization* to review, but had no room for it in his
bag and left it with me. I began to browse in it, then
settled down with the analysis of Freudian psychology which is featured there. I had been introduced
to Freud back in 1946 at Cascade Locks, Oregon,
awaiting demobilization, via *The Function of the
Orgasm* by Wilhelm Reich, but put it out of my
mind after my conversion. I had just gone through a
series of depressions, and one of the brethren suggested I seek psychiatric help. Then I got a letter
from a professor writing a book; he asked to reprint
"The Raid" and, moreover, comment on my intentions. I made to reply that it was simply "they who
live by the sword will die by the sword," but suddenly I caught myself saying "wait a minute." The
Freudian analysis was clicking in my mind. I saw
the Oedipus complex in the poem for the first time.
It was shockingly revelatory. That night a crucial
dream came and next day I began to write an erotic
fantasy of the union with the mother. In Jungian
terms, the anima invaded. But still I did not read
Jung, only Freudian books. . . . Then arrived Neu-
man's *The Origins and History of Consciousness,* which
won me over and took me back to *God and the Unconscious.* I put aside Freud and plunged into Jung. It
was now 1957.

For Everson, this return to Fr. White's study, which was to have
a central influence on the development of his thought, coin-
cided with an interest in the religious aspect of the emergence of
the Beat Generation writers, a surfacing which the poet came to
argue was in fact the reemergence in the twentieth century of
the Dionysian spirit.[4]

Because Freud's "system" is at its center atheist, it is not finally really available to Catholics; there have been, of course, attempts to bring the two programs into registration but, as Everson points out, those have ended in "the uneasy *modus vivendi* between Catholic psychiatry and Freudian psychoanalysis, based on a moot distinction between soul and psyche, wherein the mentally distressed religionist placed his immortal soul in the hand of his shrink."[5] In a paper which must have been extremely important to Everson once he began to see his newfound religious faith balanced with the perspectives of analytical psychology, "Freud, Jung and God," Fr. White argues that while Jung's split with Freud had various causes, one of the most significant was the disagreement over the nature of God and religion. "Freud's presentation of psychoanalysis," Fr. White maintains, "assumes atheism, it does not even claim to prove it." From the relatively early *Totem and Taboo* to the late *The Future of an Illusion,* Freud developed one of his central concepts—that God is simply a "fantasy substitute for the actual, and never wholly satisfactory, parent: a projection to compensate for an infantile sense of helplessness." In his later work, however, Jung argued that the inverse was true, that once we come to see Freud's notion of the sexual libido as simply a particular instance of a much more pervasive Universal Spirit, the way becomes open to us, for instance, no longer to conceive of God as a substitute for the physical father, but rather the physical father as the infant's first substitute for God, the genetically prior bearer of the image of the All-Father. God less a Big Father than the physical father a little God."[6] In short, where for Freud then religion was a symptom of psychosis, for Jung the absence of religion became the psychological disease.

A second of Fr. White's papers which certainly must have appealed to Everson was "Revelation and The Unconscious." Here Fr. White outlines the idea of prophecy and the prophet in the work of St. Thomas from an implicitly Jungian perspective. St. Thomas believed, Fr. White reminds us, in the necessity of divine revelation "because the purpose and meaning of human existence is ultimately to be found only in the invisible and incomprehensible Divinity." The nature of this purpose must, however, somehow be made manifest to us, and this is the function of prophecy. Further, Fr. White argues, St. Thomas (following St. Paul) regarded revelation as the most important of all charismata, one which "is no permanent disposition *(habitus)* to be used at will, but something momentarily undergone *(passio);* something, not that the recipient does, but that is done to him, which seizes him and overpowers him."[7]

The idea of revelation predates Christianity, of course, and Everson's sense of the prophetic voice as it relates to the function of the shaman has been abiding, informing his best essays and interviews as well as his own poetic practice since at least his conversion. "The poet knows that he speaks adequately then only when he speaks somewhat wildly," says Emerson in "The Poet," and it is the ectasy produced through controlled possession which Everson feels the shaman, like the poet, channels into artistic activity. Taking the pictographs on the cave walls of Lascaux and Almira as evidence, Andreas Lommel (whom the poet has often used as a source) judges paleolithic shamans to be the first artistically creative figures known to us.[8] Indeed, while they often functioned as physicians or high priests or priestesses, they were not simply witch doctors. Tribal witch doctors gained their status through a will to power, and were successful according to their abilities for the power of suggestion and hypnosis. Shamans, on the other hand, acted not out of a will to power but to escape from possession (or, in clinical terms, psychosis) by entering into shamanistic activity—drawing, dance, song. Thus, while in some primitive cultures shamans and witch doctors filled many of the same roles, shamans were primarily distinguished by their call to be artistically creative.

Many primitive peoples believed that through art they could influence the forces of nature. Each animal in the natural order, for example, had a "soul-force," and early hunters believed that through a painting of an animal the soul-force could be captured. Among the Ingus tribes, the word *Shingken* designated the "Lord of the Animals," a god running through all nature. It was on Shingken that the collective relied for its well-being. The shaman was entrusted with the task of interceding with Shingken to provide success in the hunt. In an ecstatic trance the shaman allowed the Lord of the Animals to enter into him, and then on his instructions an anthropomorphic idol was built under which the hunters crawled with their weapons. It was thus Shingken was captured, and the success of the hunt was assured.

As in the prophetic tradition, however, one did not become a shaman because he or she wished it, but because some mystic force compelled, and in this sense shamanism must be regarded as a vocation. In the Eskimo tradition, this outside force was called "sila," which translates literally in three ways: universe, weather, and understanding. In its religious sense, however, sila was seen as a cosmic power which invaded the shaman and in turn gave power over certain natural forces. The source of this invasion was personified as "Sila Inua, the Lord of Power," and once the shaman had been called, he or she would from that point on act as an intercessor between Sila Inua and the tribe.

In his classic study on shamanism (another Jungian influenced, crucial book for Everson), Mircea Eliade concludes that "the Dionysiac mystical current appears to have an entirely different structure" from the shamanistic mystical impulse.[9] From the point of view of the development of internal symbolism he may be correct, but in terms of defining the archetype he is, I think, mistaken. As Lommel points out, the word *shaman* itself, which has its roots in the Tungus language, designates an excited state. Like the frenzied maenads, the shaman during possession rages, undergoing bodily contortions:

> The power of shamanhood comes upon the individual like a sickness falling upon him. The individual who is destined to become a shaman feels a lassitude in his limbs that proclaims itself through violent trembling. Violent, unnatural yawning comes over him; an enormous pressure rests on his chest; he feels a sudden urge to utter violent and inarticulate cries; he is shaken by a shivering fit; he rolls his eyes, suddenly jumps up and runs around in a circle as though possessed, until he falls, bathed in sweat, and twists about on the ground in epileptic twitching and spasms.

In "The Poet as Prophet," a 1976 interview conducted by Albert Gelpi for the Lilly Foundation at Stanford University, Everson spoke at length about this subject. There he explains that the primary function of the poet as prophet is not merely to predict, but to "confront . . . to bring an awareness of transcendent value which is always the gauge by which the temporal is measured." He draws a distinction between the prophetic tradition and the shamanistic, arguing that the shaman is more likely to serve as "a living link to his reality than precipitating a confrontation with it." Still, for Everson both the prophet and the shaman (and, by extension, the poet) partake of the same archetype (St. Thomas's *passio*), and the shaman "is prophetic in the sense that he serves witness to another state of reality." Further, "the whole function of the poet as shaman is to maintain the aesthetic, not in the Modernist view, the hypothesized aesthetic object, but to maintain relevance to the archetypal world, the transcendental world, which is non-political, and sacral. It's the identity between the aesthetic and the transcendental world that is the key to the poet's prophetic function today."[10]

Everson began to solidify this view of the poet after entering the order. In his reading he "differed with Jacques Maritan and Thomas Merton who spoke of art and contemplation. Instead [he] placed art as an overflow-down rather than ascent to contemplation-up." Later, however, through Fr. White "Jung provided the archetype that gave it psychological substance" in his discussions in *Psychological Types* of the visionary, Dionysian artist. As Albert Gelpi has argued in his remarkable study of the psyche of the American poet from Taylor to Dickinson, *The Tenth Muse,* American writing has been Janus-faced from the beginning. For Gelpi, this split resides in the dichotomy between types and tropes. In Biblical exegesis, types are in essence symbols. Jonah prefigures Christ as a type of Christ, just as Abraham's legitimate son is a type of the elect, while his illegitimate son is a type of the damned. This typology becomes, Gelpi concludes, "a way of perceiving the eternal plan in the contingencies of time."[11] Conversely, tropes are creations of the human will, products of Coleridgean fancy, analogous to Wallace Stevens's "fictions." They have no transcendental dimension, no registration to the infinite "I am," but as allegory and metaphor depend for their meaning on the ingenuity and craft of their human maker.

The distinction here is between symbol and sign, *Sinnbild* and *Zeichen,* and it is at the very core of the conflict between Freudian and Jungian aesthetics. According to Jung, Freud recognized essentially no difference between symbol and sign. The Freudian symbol is equated with the "conscious contents [of the psyche] which gives us a clue to the unconscious backgrounds."[12] Symbols are therefore reduced to signs, in that for

Freud (and neo-Freudians like Rank and Jones) they are finally knowable. In this view it follows that all symbolic expressions (most especially dreams and artworks) are reducible to a dysfunction in the personal unconscious (the libido). In Freudian analysis, the patient's neurosis is thought to originate in an early trauma later repressed; it becomes the task of the therapist to recover the specific trauma and thus clear the path to regeneration of psychic balance for the patient.

While Jung agrees in part with Freud, he argues that the distinction between sign and symbol is a crucial one. "The true symbol differs essentially from [the sign], and should be understood as the expression of an intuitive perception which can as yet neither be apprehended better nor expressed differently."[13] For Jung, then, the symbol may be equated with the type; its referent, if it is to be *perceived* (rather than *created* through personal trauma), is "out-there," and its resident meanings will be a nonspecific complex. While signs may indicate dysfunction, symbols are apertures into a nonordinary reality. Unlike tropes, they are for Jung "never thought out consciously," but "always produced from the unconscious in the way of so-called revelation or intuition."[14]

In this way symbols have an exceedingly important function for they become the mediating principle between consciousness and what Jung terms the archetypes of the collective unconscious. Accepting Freud's notion of a personal unconscious composed of specifiable contents (signs) originating in a particular individual's past, Jung posits a deeper layer of the unconscious which he terms collective. The contents of this collective unconscious "do not originate in personal acquisition but in the inherited possibility of psychic functioning in general, namely, in the inherited brain-structure. These are the mythological associations—these motives and images which can spring anew in every age and clime, without historical tradition or migration."[15] In *Symbols of Transformation,* Jung details how, in conducting dream analysis of an only moderately educated patient, he was faced with symbols which bore a remarkable similarity to other more ancient and distant cultural artifacts. Because his patient could not have had previous conscious knowledge of these artifacts, Jung inferred the existence of a collective unconscious, "an inborn disposition to produce parallel images or rather identical psychic structures common to all men."[16] These psychic structures Jung calls archetypes are *a priori transpersonal dominants,* which are not specifiable signs, but rather psychic dispositions. Archetypes thus become *ways* of apprehending or intuiting as opposed to specific apprehensions or intuitions. For Jung, then, one of the central problems in the human experience resided in one's dispositions toward the objective world:

> The contents of the collective unconscious are represented in consciousness in the form of pronounced tendencies, or definite ways of looking at things. They are generally regarded by the individual as being determined by the object—incorrectly, at bottom—since they have their source in the unconscious structure of the psyche, and are only released by the operation of the object. These subjective tendencies and ideas are stronger than the objective influence; because their psychic value is higher, they are imposed upon all impressions.[17]

In *Psychological Types,* Jung discusses the problem of "pronounced tendencies" which have an extrapersonal source. He takes as an epigraph for the study a passage from Heine's *Deutschland,* in which the poet contrasts the Aristotelian and the Platonic: "These are not merely two systems, they are types of two distinct human natures, which from time immemorial, under every sort of disguise, stand more or less inimically opposed." In Jung's introduction to that volume, he explains that in his clinical work he discovered Heine's polarity to be apt, that his patients tended toward one of two attitude types: the "introverted" and the "extraverted." "The introverted attitude is characterized," he says, "by an upholding of the subject with its conscious ends and aims against the claims and pretensions of the object; the extraverted attitude, on the contrary, is distinguished by a subordination of the subject to the claims of the object."[18] This idea of an unconscious disposition which determines perception, the split between the introvert (who has a negative relationship to the object) and the extravert (who has a positive relationship to it), highlights for Jung the primary aesthetic problem, one he deals with in two extended essays, "On the Relation of Analytical Psychology to Poetic Art" and "Psychology and Literature."

There are two modes of artistic creation, Jung argues, the psychological and the visionary, and they can be differentiated according to their subject matters and their methods of creation. The psychological mode (which is tropic) draws its subject matter from the "vast realm of conscious human experience—from the vivid foreground of life." The psychological artist tends to the introverted, however, and sees his role as bringing some sort of meaning and order to this experience. His work may deal with specific political issues, more general social concerns, personal interactions, and confrontations which have their resolution on the conscious plane. The mode is psychological because it is understandable, knowable. "Even the basic experiences," Jung suggests, "though non-rational, have nothing strange about them; on the contrary, they are that which has been known from the beginning of time."[19] The artist whose disposition is toward the psychological mode sees himself primarily as a craftsman—a weaver of figures in the carpet—and this of course informs his method of creation. Because his work is "an interpretation and illumination of consciousness," his method of composition is a conscious one; that is, in his attempt to bring the objective world into clearer focus (or to create an objective world), he will remain aware of his self-imposed role as shaper and definer (or, in Robert Duncan's words, "constructivist"). In this way, the "material" of his artwork (and art is always for him a work, an arrangement) is only the "material" of his artwork. It is at all times subject to his rational, his tropic, artistic purpose. Moreover, the psychological poet, for example, will often use forms and meters as consciously imposed structuring principles, ways of ordering reality. For him a poem's form may well precede its subject, for the two are finally separable.

However, the subject matter of the visionary mode is for Jung a little more difficult to define, being "a strange something that derives its existence from the hinterland of man's mind."[20] It is symbolic, in the sense of the German *Sinnbild,* where *Sinn* conveyed some form or complex of meaning, *Bild* the thing itself, the image. The product of the symbol becomes, in alchemical terms, a *conjunctio* where the *Sinn* and the *Bild* are fused into a perfect hermaphroditus. Because for the extraverted artist, the visionary, the phenomenal world is symbolic, his art begins in the concrete, though he assumes a registration somewhere behind the curtain of appearances, a registration with the archaic and the cosmic. Where for the psychological artist consciousness is so important to his role as shaper, a giver-of-meanings, for the visionary artist consciousness is a profound stumbling block, constantly attempting to subvert his descent into the id. It becomes the task of the visionary artist to flee consciousness (and all things connected with consciousness—education and a sense of a "literary" tradition most especially) for the unconscious, flee the trope for the type. His impulse is finally not to bring order or meaning to the world, but rather to lead us to the order and meaning which reside there.

William Carlos Williams is at best a problematic figure in this context, yet he is helpful here. "Say it, no ideas but in things." Not no ideas *but* things; rather no ideas but *in* things, and this is crucial. Thus the red wheelbarrow upon which all things depend. The extravert believes he cannot shape the phenomenal world, bring his rational sense of what is or should be to it and call an order; nor does he need to. Williams is, at least in spirit if not always in practice, below it all a transcendentalist—which is, for him, the American Grain. There is an order beyond the phenomenal, and the world we experience (with the I through the eye, in Charles Olson's sense) is in registration with those eternal and perfect forms. It is not the image for Williams (and here is, it seems to me, his major split with Pound) that concerns us—not the made thing final in itself—nor the metaphoric (and here his split with the Symbolists), whose specific referent outside the trope is again a made thing, only here denying the resonance of the concrete. "Say it, no ideas but in things." Again, not no ideas, but no ideas abstracted from their source. Hence for Williams the symbolic complex: concrete phenomena—trees, chickens, a white thigh—as things which by their very concreteness are apertures into those transcendental forms, flowering into meaning. We begin with a wheelbarrow, a plum, a paper bag; we end with Whitman's leaf of grass, a notion of God.

Of all Jung's concepts, though, it is the idea of the anima/animus which has taken a central place in Everson's program; that each man carries "a spontaneous product of the unconscious" which is the feminine within him, while each woman's "unconscious has, so to speak, a masculine imprint."[21] These contra-sexual aspects, Jung argues, must be recognized and reconciled within each individual and finally, by extension, within the collective to form an androgynous whole if psychic stability is to be realized. For the eighteen and a half years Everson lived as a Dominican monk, as Brother Antoninus, almost all his work derived its substance and power from the very real tension produced by an ongoing struggle between the spirit and the flesh. *The Rose of Solitude* (1967) is probably Everson's finest achievement as Antoninus, and in the prose foreword to that book the poet recognizes this theme: "The spiritual life is both speculative and practical, but a painful tension obtains between the world of the ideal and the world of immediate experience." The subject of *Rose* is a monk's interior struggle with sexuality in his relationship with a divorced Mexican dancer. Yet even deeper, the poem sequence traces the transformation of a sexual struggle through a Jungian mergence of the masculine and feminine aspects of the Self as a path to gnosis.

In sacred literature such a theme abounds, forming, for example, the central conflicts in Augustine's *Confessions* and St. John of the Cross's Dark Night of the Soul. In our own literature, this conflict/transformation receives an early treatment in Whitman's "Children of Adam" and "Calamus." In a note, Whitman describes the idea underlying his "sex poems": "Theory of a Cluster of poems the same to the passions of Woman-love as the 'Calmus Leaves' are to adhesiveness, manly love." "Children of Adam" and "Calamus" are, in fact, celebrations of two types of human love—the passional love of man for woman and the "adhesive" love of man for man—and thus may be read as companion poems. Yet these sections offer even more than the development of the theme of celebration of the body and natural process introduced in *Song of Myself;* here the Orphic bard is transformed into the Cosmic Man, the archetypal new Adam, and we have held out to us the possibility for regeneration through the realization of our sexual nature.

"Children of Adam" opens with the identification of America as the new Eden and the poet as the new Adam, a figure who has emerged "after slumber" to "the garden of the World anew ascending." The figure of Adam is apropos here, for according to Jung "as the first man Adam is the *homo maximus*, the Anthropos, the macrocosm. He is not only the *prima materia*, but a universal soul which is also the soul of all men."[22] Where in the opening of *Song of Myself* Whitman celebrates the Self in a variety of aspects, here he focuses on "the body Electric"—"mouth, tongue, lips, teeth"—"for these are the soul." His vision is Dionysian: "Today I go consort with Nature's darlings . . . I share the midnight orgies of young men, I dance with the dancers and drink with the drinkers." "Give me the drink of my passions," Adam cries, and it is through his immersion into the world of the flesh, the world of ecstasy and spontaneity, that he returns to the peace of the primeval Garden. As Adam and Eve are paired in ecstasy so too, as Everson writes in his afterword to *River-Root,* do all men approach through sexuality regeneration and wholeness.

Yet, as Albert Gelpi has commented, "the Cosmic Man is not merely a masculine projection; he is often not only sexual but bisexual or hermaphroditic, as many images of the Self are."[23] "Children of Adam" offers us a path for regeneration through the mergence of the anima with the animus, but the psyche cannot be realized fully until the Ademic figure moves within, that is until he recognizes his own androgynous nature. This recognition occurs for Whitman in "Calamus." Historically Whitman has been chided (and more recently praised) for the homosexual overtones of "Calamus," and there is no doubt they do exist. Here the note of holiness of the body and the natural world is again struck, yet the poet's thrust seems to be away from the passional love for women to the "sturdier" and less transitory loves of "manly attachment" he sees inherent in the new Eden. "I believe the main purport of these States is to found a superb friendship," says the poet, "because I perceive it waits, and has always been waiting, latent in all men."

"Calamus" is more than a celebration of "adhesive" love between men, however, as it is in these poems that the poet allows the surfacing of the feminine aspects of his nature and thus attains the fully realized psyche of the Cosmic Man. At almost the very center of the section, Whitman writes, "Here the Frailest leaves of me and yet my strongest lasting, / Here I shade and hide my thoughts, I myself do not expose them, / And yet they expose me more than all my other poems." On one level we read this passage as the poet's confession of the dark secret of his homosexuality, yet on another Whitman is throwing over the constraints of the Apollonian for the well of the Dionysian. "Calamus" emerges not as the poet's repudiation of women, but as a recognition of the feminine within himself. Within the Cosmic Man reside both aspects of the psyche—the male and the female, the animus and the anima—and it is through sexual communion with Eve that Adam moves toward making himself whole, a process which is completed with the recognition of his androgynous nature in "Calamus."

Everson's concern with "the woman within" appears as early as the pre-Dominican, pre-Jungian *In the Fictive Wish,* though it becomes progressively more central to his poetic project through the Catholic poetry leading up to *The Rose of Solitude.* As Albert Gelpi observes, "in 'The Encounter' and several other remarkable poems towards the end of *Crooked Lines* Antoninus becomes the woman before God, his/her whole being called into activity by his totally mastering love."[24] Further, in "Annul in Me My Manhood," the poet reverses Lady Macbeth's apostrophe "unsex me here," asking that God might make him "woman-sexed and weak, / if by that total transformation / I might know Thee more," while the later "God Germed in Raw Granite" asks "Is this she? Woman within / . . . when we / Well-wedded merge, by Him / Trained into one and solved there." But it is not until *Rose* that Everson moves beyond a sense of the recognition of the anima as a facet of his quest, like Whitman, to a realization that in fact the woman within is its object.

The Prologue to *Rose* announces that volume's theme, one that parallels Whitman's while significantly altering its situation in that here the struggle is overtly male-female:

> The dark roots of the rose cry in my heart.
> They pierce through rock-ribs of my stony flesh
> Invest the element, the loam of life.
> They twist and mesh.
>
> The red blood of the rose beats on, beats on,
> Of passion poured, of fiery love composed,
> Virtue redeemed, the singular crest of life,
> And pride deposed.
>
> Love cries regenerate and lust moans consumed,
> Shaken in terror on that rage of breath.
> Untrammeled still the red rose burns on
> And knows no death.
>
> Petal by crimson petal, leaf by leaf,
> Unfolds the luminous core, the bright abyss,
> Proffers at last the exquisite delight
> Of the long kiss.
>
> Until shall pass away the wasted means
> Leaving in essence what time held congealed:
> The Sign of God evoked from the splendid flesh
> Of the rose revealed.

The opening lines of the poem present a traditional symbol, though the situation is ambiguous: we have a rose (and we think here of Dante or, perhaps because the "roots" are "dark," of Blake or Roethke), yet at the same instant the rose seems to be a thing both external to the poet (i.e., a woman) and part of him as well. The question becomes one of direction—is the rose something that has invaded him (his infatuation with an Other) or is it something already resident in the poet, buried deep in his soul, crying to emerge? Because Antoninus's affair with Rose Tunneland, the divorced Mexican dancer, occasions the poem, the first possibility seems the obvious. However, the first line is telling: the rose is crying in his heart; that is, we do not necessarily have a movement inward "through rock-ribs" of "stony flesh," but possibly a movement outward to the "loam of life" which is psychic wholeness. In this sense, the rose becomes symbolic of the poet's feminine aspect, and the movement of the poem, the unfolding "petal by crimson petal, leaf by leaf" of the rose, becomes as much a figurative enactment of the poet's emerging recognition of his own androgynous nature as a specifically sexual circumstance. On the one hand, the monk finds in the body of his woman "The Sign of God"; on the other, it is the "splendid flesh of the Rose" of his anima which reveals to him the core of his religion and affords him regeneration.

Throughout the sequence's five sections, Whitman's Adam is transformed into the Christ-figure, the poet crucified, having nailed himself "to the Mexican cross, / The flint knife of her beauty." Of course, such symbolism is perhaps rather unextraordinary given Everson's situation—a monk whose vow of celibacy is undergoing a rigorous test—but it works on a level deeper than the immediate. According to Jung's studies the cross (which is a primary symbol in *Rose*) "is a many-faceted symbol, and its chief meaning is that of the 'tree of life' and the 'mother,' certainly an instrument of pain, but one leading to regeneration."[25] Further, Christ's crucifixion (which the poet here reenacts in the passion of his own life) is often identified with a passing into androgyny. In his *Sermo Suppositus* Augustine writes: "Like a bridegroom Christ went forth from his chamber, he sent out with a presage of his nuptials into the field of the world. . . . He came to the marriage-bed of the cross, and there, in mounting it, he consummated his marriage. And when he perceived the sighs of the creature, he lovingly gave himself up to the torment in place of his bride, and he joined himself to the woman forever."[26]

Jung points out that the sense of the Christ figure himself as androgynous has played a crucial role in the Christian tradition, relating specifically to the Adamic myth: "the Church symbolism of *sponsus* and *sponsa* leads to the mystic union of the two, i.e., to the anima Christi which lives in the *corpus mysticism* of the Church. This unity underlies the idea of Christ's androgyny . . . which is no doubt connected with the Platonic conception of the bisexual First Man, for Christ is ultimately the Anthropos."[27]

In *Aion,* Jung goes on to remind us that iconography often pictures Christ with breasts (in the manner of "The New Birth" from the *Rosarium philosophorum secunda pars alchimiae de lapide philosophico,* Frankfurt, 1550) "in accordance with the Song of Solomon 1:1 'For thy breasts are better than wine.'"[28] Finally, the "symbol of the hermaphrodite, it must be remembered, is one of the many synonyms for the goal of the art" of alchemy, which like poetry seeks to reunite the contradictions of the fallen phenomenal world into their primal unity.[29]

The scandal surrounding the publication of *The Rose of Solitude* in the more conservative quarters of the Church can thus be seen as a reaction not so much to the situation of the sequence (in 1967 a narrative of a monk's fall, especially a felix culpa, would raise few eyebrows), but rather in the Lawrentian implications of Everson's erotic vision:

My act lives.

From its life delivered
I stand free.

Of the Rose renewed
I rise, I rise,
I stand free.

In the wisdom of the flesh,
In the truth of the touch,
In the silence of the smile
Redeemed.

("Immortal Strangeness")

And further,

I have said before:
All the destinies of the divine
In her converge.

To love her more
Is to love self less
And to love self less
Is to love God more.

To love selflessly
Is to love:

Him in her.

Amen.

("On the Thorn")

As the Christ figure, Everson, like Whitman's Anthropos, finds regeneration not in mortification and denial. Rather, as these powerful poems trace the poet's sexual dark night in his conflict with the flesh, it is finally his submission to his passion for the Rose—the woman within—which affords him wholeness: "When the devil / Can't find a way / He sends a woman. / So does God."

The influence of Jung, then, both on Everson's sense of the poet's mission and on his writing from the Catholic period especially has been profound. I do not mean to imply, however, that Everson is a mere epigone, an apologist in verse for Jungian thought. Poets as diverse as Robert Creeley, Robert Duncan, and Denise Levertov have asserted the romantic notion of the poem as "given," of course, and thus have aligned themselves at least to an extent with the shamanistic tradition. Among postwar poets of consequence, however, only Allen Ginsberg, it seems to me, matches Everson's enduring trust in the poet's prophetic vocation. For Everson, this trust was, if not discovered, at least confirmed and deepened greatly through his contact with analytical psychology. Further, through longterm study of Jung's basic concepts, Everson was able in poems like *The Rose of Solitude* sequence and *River-Root* to explore more fully the rather dark and dangerous territory opened in American poetry by Whitman and thus settle on what has come to be his overriding concern—the reconciliation of the anima and the animus as the salvific principle.

3 ☀ "The Constant Exchange Rendered True": The Later Robert Duncan

1.   *The Ground of* Ground Work

> In periods of the greatest panic, such as the eighteenth century following the nightmare religious enthusiasms and wars of the seventeenth, the form tolerable to convention can shrink to a tennis court.
>
> The Truth and Life of Myth

"In writing I came to be concerned not with poems in themselves but with the life of poems as part of the evolving and continuing work of a poetry I could never complete—a poetry that had begun long before I was born and that extended beyond my own work in it. . . . I strove for the quality of my participation in the art" ("Man's Fulfillment in Order and Strife").

2/3/88. Bill Everson called from Davenport this morning to say that both Robert Duncan and Adrian Wilson had died, within an hour of each other.

I met Wilson, one of our finest printers (he had finished a lovely edition of *In Medias Res* a year before) at Everson's in

1986, with his wife, Joyce. We talked for an afternoon about the Waldport c.o. camp (where he'd been interned during the war with Everson), the Bay Area printing and art scene, theater. It was the same afternoon that I spoke to Duncan on the phone about the *Sagetrieb* letters.

I met Duncan twice. First (May 1980), at UC Davis, where I was teaching as a lecturer, after completing my doctoral work. Chris Wagstaff had arranged the reading, which was, as usual with Duncan (and Olson, and Everson), a talk. Dressed in (what looked to be an expensive) three-piece, pin-striped suit, he read a few poems from a notebook, but concentrated mainly on an energetic consideration of alchemy, ranging through Hermes Trismegistus, the Kabala, Blake, the gnostic gospels; dismissing Jung and, especially, the notion of archetypes as reductive. After just over two and a half hours of monologue, Duncan finished up, sensing our intellectual exhaustion, a kindness as he was obviously just warming to his subject. We all moved to a restaurant off campus for dinner, where he signed my copies of *Roots and Branches, Bending the Bow*. There, after a few drinks, someone asked him what he thought about "deep image." "How deep?" he shot back. "An inch? A foot? All the way to China?"

The other instance was in November 1985, speaking with Duncan and Jack Gilbert at the Ezra Pound Conference in San Jose. He opened the conference the first night with a reading from *Ground Work, Before the War,* his first new book in over fifteen years, and from new poems which would go to make up *Ground Work II, In the Dark*. I remember especially the intimate and agonized final poem, "After A Long Illness," the poem that would soon close his last volume, addressed to his companion Jess: "in the dark this state / that knows nor sleep nor waking, nor dream / —an eternal arrest." That night he finished in well under an hour, trembling.

On the next morning's panel Duncan was almost himself again, animated and animating; his red suspenders were a nice touch. He spoke of his respect for Pound and Williams and Stein and H.D. He mentioned the kidney illness and the weirdness of dialysis, life in the Bay Area in the forties, Freud. After the discussion, he asked me about Everson's Parkinson's, suggested he would try to get down to see him (which some months later, with Albert Gelpi, he did). He wrote a few lines in my notebook, in a weak, almost illegible hand:

> At the curtain   hearing a voice
>   from which   who hears
> listens?
>
>   we   weavers of the curtain
>   need
> the weaving voices
>   in extemity
> moving   the dark again.

He published little ("I do not intend to issue another collection of my work since *Bending the Bow* until 1983 at which time fifteen years will have passed," *Caesar's Gate,* 1972) during the last two decades of his life, though he lived to see the Ekbert Faas biography (1983), *Ground Work* (1984, a year later than he planned), *Fictive Certainties* (1985), and Robert Bertholf's magnificent bibliography (1986) into print, as well as an advance, specially bound copy of *Ground Work II.*

"The life of poems as part of the continuing, evolving work."

Both *Ground Work I* and *II* (Kenneth Irby points out that originally Duncan had intended the title to be *Transmissions*) continue to explore the formal possibilities of the field. The typography of the first volume especially seems of crucial concern, prefaced as it is by "some notes on notation" and reproduced from Duncan's own typescript, politics (and the whole question of the artist as a political conscience), allusion and derivation, collage, self, and perception.

Architecture. Before the Dark includes work from *Bending the Bow* (1968) through 1975: sets include additions to *Passages* and *Structure of Rime, Poems from the Margins of Thom Gunn's Moly* (1972), *A Seventeenth Century Suite in Homage to the Metaphysical Genius in English Poetry* (1973), and the *Dante Etudes* (published as *Dante* in 1974. In my copy he has added in holograph "radical, liberal" to the epigraph, which is corrected here.) There are also additional shards. *In the Dark:* post 1975; more from *Passages* (especially "Regulators") and *Structure of Rime* ("The Five Songs"); sets: "An Alternative Life," "To Master Baudelaire," "Veil, Turbine, Cord & Bird."

Typography. The physicality of the thing, the dance. Duncan, 1956: "This is a dance in whose measured steps time emerges, as space emerges from the dance of the body. The ear is intimate to muscular equilibrium" ("Regarding Olson's Maximus"). Duncan, 1984: "The cadence of the verse, and, in turn, the interpenetration of cadences in sequence is, for me, related to the dance of my physical body" (*Ground Work I*).

> *Lovely their feet pound the green solid meadow.*
>   *The dancers*
> *mimic flowers—root stem stamen and petal*
>   *our words are,*
> *our articulations, our*
>   *measures.*

The sounding of the measure, the voice of it, the music, effecting Olson's summons in "Projective Verse" (1950): "It is time we picked the fruits of the experiments of Cummings, Pound, Williams, each of whom has, after his way, already used the machine as a scoring to his composing, as a script to its vocalization . . . as though not the eye but the ear was to be its measurer."

In his notes on Olson's *Maximus,* Duncan is explicit in his attention to the oral: " 'By ear, he sd.' This is the beginning point (as the discrimination of speech). But, if the muscular realization [McClure: "Poetry is a muscular principle"] of language is the latest mode of poetry, the beginning point was muscular too, localized in the discharges of energy expressed in the gaining, first, breath, and then, tongue. The gift of spirit and of tongues."

(Having been, mostly, a thousand miles from San Francisco for nearly a decade, I heard of the run-ins between Duncan and a few of the San Francisco "Language poets" only secondhand—Duncan telling one at a conference, for example, to "get off the stage." [To McClure: "Let us take a really 'jerk' poetry, like Language poetry is to my mind," *Conjunctions* 7.] I assume he felt [I think, at times, perhaps wrongly] a poem like Barrett Watten's "Decay" to be without music, without "tongue"; for his part, Watten overheard at the SF MLA Conference [1987], "Duncan is not a cognitive poet," which was not, to my mind, a compliment. Even so, Duncan respected greatly Michael Palmer's project, and was a source for him. And Ron Silliman has written sympathetically of Duncan, calling him [in *Maps*] "thoroughly a creature of the auditory imagination" for whom "sounds suggest solutions, *are,* in fact, his way of making decisions within the writing.")

One of the primary threads of *Ground Work I, Before the War* is further exploration of—and insistence on—the oral. The opening "Some Notes on Notation" says, flatly, that "all 'typographical' features are notations for the performance of the reading" (whether, I take it, out loud or inner-vocalized. An earlier instance of such a typographically articulated stratagem appears in *Bending the Bow*.) Thus (especially in the "Passages") "I have workt with silences"—the *caesura* ([<=*caes* {*us*} cut {ptp. of *caedere*} {*caed-* cut + −*tus* ptp. suffix} + −*ura*-ure]) becomes a major feature, indicating as it does a duration, a breakage:

> *dying upward,   giving way*

Duncan's use of the caesura (signalled by a double space after a comma), however, is more than that. Traditionally (or even in his contemporary James Dickey, *The Eye-Beaters*), the caesura serves as a kind of punctuation, a secondary feature which offers a dramatic emphasis to the primary movement of the line, and certainly, to an extent, Duncan's caesura functions in that minor capacity. More crucially, though, Duncan's emphasis on the "silence" for which the caesura or "white space" serve as notation, consciously echos John Cage's more profound sense of that which is "called silence only because it does not form part of a [traditional] musical intention" ("Silence"). The absence of presence, the presence of absence; Roland Barthes (*Elements of Semiology*): "*a significant absence,*" a phrase the poet himself takes in his preface—"Silence itself is sounded, a significant or meaningful absence, its semiotic value contributing to and derived from our apprehension of the field of the poem it belongs to. . . . Silences themselves as phrases, units in the measure, charged with meaning." *Charged with meaning,* both in terms of emphasis and, as with Cage, of allowing the world itself to pass in and out of the poem. The work becomes simultaneously a construction and a found thing, an ongoing interweaving constantly calling attention to both instances of convergence and irreconcilable distance.

(Duncan came to know Cage's work through Olson and

Black Mountain; "Duncan is an immensely facile man, one who seems to live Cage's theories on the simultaneity of diverse actions" [Duberman, *Black Mountain*].)

Thus Duncan: "So what was interesting to me was that a dance was beginning to emerge in which all the dancers cooperate. That is to say, they had to be attentive to where they were. Similarly, in Cage's music, you cannot presume a melody. So if you aren't hearing it, then you simply aren't. . . . What attracted me to this aleatoric music was a potential recognition that there was something else than the neo-Platonic scale out of which we get all our sense of harmony that has dominated music for so long. Instead of that, we get a larger picture in which every conceivable sound is present. And now we find that our original harmonies don't disappear as being present, but they are co-present with all the other elements, and we have to be attentive throughout" (Faas, *Towards A New American Poetics*).

Further, the employment of a caesura activates a suspension of the "syntactic bond" between various phrases.

"Did I want so to come into the question of an abyss of feeling? The whole company dancing I went round from dancer to dancer as if the Presence of the Dance were everywhere there beckoning, alluring. Each place a lure for me" (*Ground Work I*).

"A sounded silence," he writes in the opening notes, and "margins signify." He even invents a particular code to indicate stanzaic breaks when such come at the end of a page so that there can be no mistaking. Again and again throughout the volume the question of the oral is, as it has always been in his work, emphasized: "A Song From the Structures of Rime Ringing as the Poet Paul Celan Sings," "speaking in tongues," "a vocal chord in the throat before Time, / from which the consciousness and dissonances of lives vibrate," "it was a wounded mouth, / a stricken thing unable to release its word," "Our Art but to Articulate," "Songs of an Other," the final "Circulations of the Song." The "music of men's speech," he reflects in "Towards an Open Universe," has "its verity in the music of the inner structure of Nature," as does mathematics. And the poem, "the instrument of music that [the poet] makes from men's speech, has such a hunger to live, to be true, as mathematics has."

"Notes on the Structure of Rime" (for Warren Tallman, spring 1961): "Poetry, like painting, sculpture, architecture, music or dance, is not essentially dependent on writing, for the arts are born in a memorization. . . . It does not *sound* like what it says, Jess remarks of some poetries. . . . In the realized poem, the poem that is *sound* thruout, the poet attends even as we do the order of what the poem is saying. . . . Thru and thru this Mass of the Performance of Telling, the heart, the breath, the mouth, the tongue articulating, the entire attention of the whole was to the World in Creation there" (*Maps* 6).

One of Duncan's fullest expressions of such questions as orality and notation (along with some useful autobiographical instances of his practical problems with publishers and printers) appears in the special Duncan issue of *Maps* (6, 1974; John Taggart, ed.). There he reprints a note which appears in the booklet reproducing pages from his notebook and typescript which accompanied *Tribunals: Passages 31–35* (1970), and which aggressively offers his sense of the script as "score," with particular reference to the typewriter and its own special spacings and relationships on the page. "The typed copy is for me the primary 'score' of the poem, and the printed version (*though not this printed version*) subject to close-space conventions of modern printing, in striving for a homogenized density of type on the page against open spaces, rides over decisions that appear in the typed version as notation of the music of the poem, minute silences in the space after a comma or a period." He concludes by drawing from Olson's "Projective Verse" perhaps the first extended treatment of the profound effect of the typewriter on the process of composition: "It is the advantage of the typewriter that, due to its rigidity and its space precisions, it can, for a poet, indicate exactly the breath, the pauses, the suspensions even of syllables, the juxtapositions even of parts of phrases, which he intends."

Duncan's troubles with printers were significant; not only were his spacings constantly violated, but incredibly, for example, Graham Mackintosh dropped twenty-four lines from "The Christ in the Olive Grove" in *Bending the Bow* in order to end with a proper page count. (Across my study I am looking at a copy of my own edition of Everson's selected essays and interviews, *Earth Poetry*, which Mackintosh printed for Oyez; I was living in Bordeaux during the process, saw no proof, and the first *paragraph* of my preface contains *four* significant typographical errors, including "xor" for "for" and, now at a distance amusingly, spelling Everson "Everyon.")

In 1971, Duncan privately published a multilithed *Ground Work* in an edition of 400 copies, consisting of a one-page prospectus and twelve pages of text drawn from his notebooks. There he announced his intention that "a volume of passages from notebooks current and old, poems in progress and previously unedited poems, starts and fits, drawing and propositions" since *Bending the Bow* would be published "once something like a hundred pages has been done" in a similar "immediate" copy by subscription. This project never appeared, but when *Ground Work I* was published by New Directions thirteen years later, it was offset from Duncan's own typescript, for the first time in a major book allowing him complete control over typography. Even so, in his *Bibliography* Bertholf lists seven errors in the text, including the dropping of six lines in "Coda" to "A Seventeenth Century Suite."

Ground Work II, while retaining the wide format, is set in type. Peter Glassgold, who saw the book through New Directions: "Robert's health was failing badly and there was an aura of mortality about the poems. . . . Robert Bertholf, who had been taking care of all literary matters for Robert for the past couple years, brought him *In the Dark,* and it is some consolation that he was perfectly, wonderfully pleased with it" (*American Poetry,* 1988).

(Spring, 1985. Letter from Tom Parkinson, calling for signatures for awarding Duncan the first National Poetry Award "for his lifetime devotion to the art of poetry and his grand achievement culminating in the publication of *Ground Work, Before the War.*" The book was overlooked by the various traditional literary awards, as well as the *New York Times Book Review.* Members of Parkinson's board: Creeley, Davidson, Di Prima, Everson, Ferlinghetti, Gunn, McClure, and Reed. Three hundred poets and critics contributed funds for the prize, signed the scroll. George Bowering, in a letter from Canada, "In our country there are three generations of poets who write as if Robert Duncan were the great teacher.")

Derivation. Duncan, frankly, and contra–Bloom's notion of the anxiety of influence: "I was, after all, to be a poet of many derivations" (*The Years As Catches*). Thus, for example, *Ground Work*'s "A Seventeenth Century Suite" offered "in homage" to the metaphysicals "being imitations, derivations & variations upon certain conceits and findings made among strong lines."

(As *Writing Writing* [1964] imitated Stein, or, in 1940, sending William Everson typescripts of his attempt to [re] write *Hamlet;* a full collection of *Derivations* was published in 1969 by Fulcrum Press, London.) The act of writing becomes (as in the case of Michael Palmer) an act of close reading, and even more crucially the act of reading becomes a generative process, so that (as in "A Poem Beginning with a Line by Pindar") the earlier texts become initiatory. Duncan's "Poems from the Margins of Thom Gunn's *Moly*" quote Gunn or directly, or allude, or rewrite:

Gunn: Something is taking place.
        Horns bud bright in my hair.
        My feet are turning hoof.
        And Father, see my face
        —Skin that was damp and fair
        Is barklike and, feel, rough.

Duncan: Something is taking place.
        Horns thrust upward from the brow.
        Hooves beat impatient where feet once were.
        My son, youth grows alarming in your face.
        Your innocent regard is cruelly charming to me now.
        You bristle where my fond hand would stir
        to stroke your cheek.   I do not dare.

Duncan's poem is occasioned by Gunn's (whose in turn had been occasioned by Homer's); it repeats certain phrases, offers variations on others, adds what is needed. Throughout, in changing the voice from the son's to the father's (to an extent this is the older Duncan speaking to the younger Gunn), Duncan offers as answer to Gunn a reinscription of his own reinscription of Homer.

Originality was never a question; it was, rather, a hindrance to the ongoing project of Poetry: "It is the originality of

Pound that mars his intelligence. The goods of the intellect are communal; there is a *virtu* or power that flows from the language itself, a fountain of man's meanings, and the poet seeking the help of this source awakens first to the guidance of those who have gone before in the art, then the guidance of the meanings and dreams that all who ever stored the honey of the invisible in the hive have prepared" (*HD Book*).

(In biology, derivation denotes the theory of evolution of organic forms.)

By embracing derivation as a given, Duncan manages to move beyond the question of "anxiety of influence," freely dipping at any moment into the cultural "honey of the invisible," acting as both commentator and (re)storer. Like a later oral poet telling the *Iliad,* his presence is a vortex, as he becomes a kind of animated and creative reference librarian to our cultural store, his body of work a living museum.

> It is the architecture then of arts inspired by confidences
> of an earthquake yet to come. The Muses are of stone
>   to be riven
> from stone. And they dream—it is the vision of this
>   very art in
> which, out of no confidence, their confidential song
>   comes into me—
> into the abyss they gaze
> into which the Museum falls. ("The Museum")

A magpie's nest. Duncan's stepfather was an architect, as, in a sense, was his "poetry stepfather," Pound. Although "originality mars his intelligence," *The Cantos* "are ever-present form. . . . Ezra Pound has never failed me as a model; I mean he is still my master. And a master is someone that in every sense is your master" (Ginsberg, *Allen Verbatim*).

Discussing Pound's sense of the ideogram in *The Truth and Life of Myth,* Duncan argues that "the work of art is itself the field we would render the truth of. Focusing in on the process itself as the field of the poem, the jarring discord must enter the composition." Reference here specifically to Olson ("We now enter, actually, the large area of the whole poem, into the FIELD, if you like, where all the syllables and all the lines must be managed in their relations to each other," "Projective Verse") and Whitehead ("But in analysis it can only be understood as a process, that is to say in passage," *Process and Reality*).

Olson: "Duncan never has any trouble stealing because he has a visional experience which prompts him to reach out for just what he knows he wants" ("Causal Mythology"). For Duncan, Olson's "field" metaphor is appropriate but his definition too exclusive, dividing as it does the "projective" from the "nonprojective," a subject he has remarked on in numerous places: "I want to keep the whole thing going, so although I'm not going to take Charles' alternatives, I'm not going to take closed form versus the open form because I want both, and I'll make open forms that have closed forms in them and closed forms that are open. . . . Here I think there is a field. And if there is a field of poetry, then this is all one" (Bowering and Hogg "Interview"). Or, as he tells Faas re: Olson, "Would you want to go back and correct, let's say, Houseman?" (To an extent, I suppose, much of Duncan's work post-1955 can be read as an ongoing dialogue with Olson.)

"Only Charles and I seem to have field theory," he told Faas. "And we are the only ones after all from the thirties when Koehler's field theory was very exciting. Koehler's field theory of the aesthetics of painting and his attempt to read music that way." Michael Davidson points out that Duncan's pre-Olson reading included not only Koehler's *The Place of Value in World of Facts,* but Norbert Wiener's *Cybernetics* and Siegfried Giedion's *Mechanization Takes Command,* proving, along with Stravinsky and Schoenberg, "paradigms for systems of interrelated parts directed toward the coherence of the whole" (*Scales of the Marvellous*, ed. Bertholf and Reid). Further, the generative possibilities of the "serial poems" of Jack Spicer and Robin Blaser. "Passages 33":

> Not one but many energies shape the field.
> It is a vortex. It is a compost.

Pound spoke of *The Cantos* as a ragbag, Duncan (in *The Years As Catches*) of his own work as "a magpie's nest or a collage, a construct of disparate elements drawn into the play they have excited, a syncretic religion." Poems like *Passages* and *Structure of Rime* (his first serial poem), unlike *The Cantos*, say, or *Paterson*, are run over the course of many books, culminating in *Ground Work*, their sections interspersed among other poems. "The life of poems as part of the continuing, evolving work." He tells Bowering and Hogg, "My concept of form is the coherence of all parts and all other parts . . . so a poem is discovering the actuality of the form it is anyway, it is the consciousness in its composition, the indwelling in and discovering the form that's there."

("My thought as a poet has grown in the ground of twentieth-century mythologists like Cassier and Freud, found a key in Jane Harrison's definition of the dithyramb as 'the song that makes Zeus leap or beget,' and followed the mythopoeic weavings of Pound's *Cantos* in which 'all ages are contemporaneous,'" *The Truth and Life of Myth*. Whitehead, in his description of duration [*Concept of Nature*], concludes that "simultaneity is a definite natural relation.")

Duncan is drawn in 1951 to Jess Collins as an artist/lover, writes many notes to Jess's "picture books." For Jess, the collagist (his collage is reproduced on the cover of *Ground Work I*), "Every point of color is autonomous, but still it is within the total relationship, the total network of color," the field (*Translation*).

Wittgenstein: "The work of the philosopher consists in assembling reminders *for* a particular purpose." Duncan: To *reveal* a particular purpose. "Central to a defining of the poetics I am trying to suggest here is the conviction that the order man may contrive or impose upon the things about him or upon his own language is trivial beside the divine order or natural order he may discover in them." Duncan dismisses Pound's "and I cannot make it cohere" of "Canto 116" in favor of "SPLEN-DOUR, IT ALL COHERES" of his *The Women of Trachis* (*Bending the Bow*). Following Whitehead, Duncan's version of the world, version of art, is romantic, as the poet emerges not as a giver of meanings but a revealer of them: "The artist, after Dante's poetics, works with all parts of the poem as *polysemous,* taking each thing of the composition as generative of meaning, a response to and a contribution to the building form. The old doctrine of correspondences is enlarged and furthered in a new process of responses."

A new *process* of responses. Duncan—Whitehead / Pound—Fenollosa and the question of process. Hugh Kenner: Fenollosa's "unassailable originality stemmed from his conviction that the unit of thought was less like a noun than like a verb, and that Chinese signs therefore denoted processes" (*The Pound Era*). In Whitehead's sense, process and existence "presuppose each other," and thus the notion of a fixed point (a static version of the image) is fallacious in that we can only come to regard such an occurrence in the context of an ongoing flux. We have, as example, not only the poems but the ongoing *H.D. Book* which, like *Passages,* is scattered throughout various journals (many ephemeral) not necessarily in sequential order. Duncan's reading of this Imagist as fluid, underscoring the necessity of reflection/refraction in the field. Even there the method is "grand collage."

To Robin Blaser, 1957: "The field as the ground as well as the field of vision, is constant. And that the total work is another field, as one works in writing as one's field" (*Ironwood*). The *field* as the *ground*. Thus, *The Opening of the Field;* thus, *Ground Work. Before the War,* as both prior to and standing before (standing, Duncan to McClure, "before the mirror"; looking in the mirror [Whitehead, *Process and Reality*] we see both the illusion of the object and the landscape behind—"it thereby defines a cross-section of the universe"). *In the Dark,* as it surrounds; or, *Bending the Bow,* "In the poem this very lighted room is *dark,* and the *dark* alight with love's intentions. *It* is striving to come into existence in these things, or, all striving to come into existence is It–in this realm of men's languages a poetry of all poetries, *grand collage,* I name It."

So that:

> "I have given you a cat in the dark," the voice said.
> Everything changed in what has always been there
> at work in the Ground: the two titles
>   "Before the War," and now, "In the Dark"
> underwrite the grand design.   The magic
>   has always been there,   the magnetic purr
>   run over me, the feel as of cat's fur
> charging the refusal to feel.   That black stone,
>   now I see, has its electric familiar.

2.   *On Duncan: A Talk With William Everson*

Robert Duncan died February 3, 1988, following a long illness. A number of writers agreed to write brief essays on the poet for a special issue of *American Poetry,* including William

Everson. Due to his long trial with Parkinson's disease, however, Everson was unable to complete his tribute. In its place he agreed to discuss his friend with me at his home in the Santa Cruz Mountains on March 8, 1988.

What I was particularly impressed with about Duncan's death was the prestige he had accumulated over the last years of his life. This was apparent in the acclaim and homage occasioned by his passing. The front page of the *San Francisco Chronicle,* no less. I hadn't expected that. No matter how much coterie-support we poets can count on, we hardly think of ourselves as front page news.

How did you regard his reputation?

Well, over the years we were always under a cloud from the establishment—disparaged as bohemians, beatniks, and hippies. What seems to have happened is with the passing of all the great modernists, and now with the second generation almost gone, Duncan emerges in prime place, with impeccable credentials, as a foreward carrier of consciousness, the bearer of those celebrated values.

So you place Duncan in the modernist line.

Emphatically. Following Pound, he was a long-time, banner-bearing member, and so built his career. Then in the Faas interview he reversed himself and claimed romanticism. I think he was probably disassociating himself from the oppressive postmodernist sweep, which has become so total it chiefly inspires tedium. The truth probably is that in his head he was a modernist but in his heart of hearts he was a romanticist. Actually the position isn't all that common. Al Gelpi's new book, *A Coherent Splendor,* is a masterful study of the prolongation of romanticist values in the marrow of the modernist bone. However, if the Augustan age can be thought of as the thesis, due to the establishment of a self-conscious formal English literature, and the romantic revolt taken as the antithesis, then modernism shapes up in a fairly creditable synthesis. I say "fairly creditable" because Gelpi stresses what pains the modernist masters took to disparage romanticism. But it doesn't look like we're headed for another thesis, a new Augustan Age. On the contrary, it looks like Robert's instinct will prove correct: full speed ahead to neoromanticism! And he brings a special proclivity to the synthesis, possessing almost a physical disposition in the upshot. I have in mind the childhood accident to his eyes, which left him cross-eyed, bifurcating his vision, making him more aware of accidentals than of essences, or at least more than people of normal vision.

Can you explain this a little more fully, how this applies to modernism over against romanticism?

The thrust of romanticism was toward the sublime but by the century's close it had deteriorated to the banal, giving the new century, our own, the opportunity to emerge as a quasi-classical hegemony called modernism, in which intangibles like complexity and abstraction, sophisticated technical invention and spatialized form, take precedence over the substantive rendition of the subject in romanticism's preoccupation with strong emotional resonance of the ideal. Thus Robert's eye injury with its consequent bifurcation put him in line with the aesthetic abstraction that was modernism's special characteristic. In the same way an artist hooked on drugs may find his imbalance inadvertently increases his penetration into the rarified interstices of a disordered world. Actually, Ekbert Faas goes into it in the opening pages of his biography of Duncan, giving Robert's own version of his weird vision and goes on to speculate that the eye defect may well have had its positive effects for a child who was to face multiple alienation as orphan, sexual deviant, and disreputable bohemian.

Who were Duncan's primary modernist precursors?

Ezra Pound and William Carlos Williams.

And romantics?

Coleridge, I would assume. He wasn't particularly Wordsworthian.

But you seem to regard the modernist impulse to hold the primary position.

Without doubt, over the greater part of his career Robert was a torchbearer for the modernist movement, a front-runner for an entire field this is passing away. Even its sequel, postmodernism, is finished. The new romanticism is emerging not out of literature as yet but out of popular culture—namely, the New Age. The literary movement will surface later when the intellectual elite gets accustomed to it, which will take some time, because the snobs did not discover it themselves, so they stand aloof. But they'll come around. Never forget the three stages of an idea: first, it's false, heresy, a lie; second, it may not be false but it is irrelevant; and three, "But we knew that all the time!"

I think Robert knew in his bones that postmodernism was finished; it was so widespread, so universally followed that it had become predictable. So he started back to the fountainhead. But he did not live long enough to do much with it, and maybe it's just as well he completes his witness with his modernist achievement intact. His life is more coherent this way.

What do you think is his greatest attribute?

His visionary insight into the intangible dimension of phenomena constituting reality, and the imagination to register it in graphic figures and potent speech. He had a marvellous sense of imagery, but went too much by aesthetic theory, which seems the modernist pitfall. Modernist art becomes too esoteric, too abstract. It eschews the common touch, the physical dimension. Duncan was a seeker. His life, his art was a quest. All his experimentation was a search for the will o' the whisp of significance in the welter of circumstance. His whole life was a record of sojourning in one or another branch of aesthetic speculation. When he was working out one of these phases he often wrote poems that were not very interesting. To him they were vital, because the search was vital, and to many postmodernists they were ingenious and hence commendable; but as poetry they were too abstract. Then when he had the implications worked out he would stop to catch his breath, and the span of his attention would drop below the speculative level to the old inveterate lizard waiting with primordial patience in the heart of man, or in his plexus, his groin. And it will rouse itself, wake from its long hibernation, and slit its skin lids, and sing. And the libidinous song will find his lips, and its thin reptillian croon run down his arm to his fingerling pen, and the song of salvation is born again, the litany of self-renewal is heard again in the world:

> Negroes, negroes, all those princes,
> holding cups of rinoceros bone, make
> magic with my blood. Where beautiful Marijuana
> towers taller than the eucalyptus, turns
> within the lips of night and falls,
> falls downward, where as giant Kings we gathered
> and devourd her burning hands and feet, O Moonbar
> thee and Clarinet! Those talismans
> that quickened in their sheltering leaves like thieves,
> those Negroes, all those princes

holding to their mouths like Death
the cups of rhino bone,
were there to burn my hands and feet.
divine the limit of the bone and with their magic
tie and twist me like a rope. I know
no other continent of Africa more dark than this
dark continent of my breast.

Once the theoretical problem was worked out he would return to a more integrative poetry. At that point the mood changed from intellectual quest to visceral recovery, maybe for only a single poem, essentially out of sequence, but fundamental.

Would he have thought of himself as a vatic poet?

That was his pride, his sense of vocation.

Why would he be so drawn to H. D.?

Her modernist sensibility. Actually, he was always attracted to intellectual women. Unlike many homosexuals he was not a misogynist. But he had enough of it in him that he wasn't cowed by militant feminists, as I am. I've thanked my stars for his presence more than once, on some university panel when my sexist poetry of an earlier day was in hot water. Sexism and violence coexist in the masculine unconscious, as they do in the feminine, and to get at them you have to expose them. This is best done through your art. Duncan understood the function of the violence in what I was doing. He would stop an incensed feminist in her tracks with, "Have you ever been raped? No? Well, I have. I didn't enjoy it, but I understood what was happening and why. And it was not without its value." As for H. D., her modernist credentials were impeccable. She was the first Imagist. That in itself would be enough to quicken Duncan's interest. Actually, Gelpi's book is very convincing on

H.D. as a vatic poet in her own right. But Duncan's esteem for latter-day postmodernist male poets is harder for me to understand. They had the vatic impulse but lacked the means.

What about Charles Olson?

I could never grasp what Robert saw in Olson's versecraft, his technique. I never thought of him as all that much of a poet. In his Faas interview, Gary Snyder said much the same thing: how, when Olson made his appearance on the San Francisco scene, he provoked interest as a commentator or historian, rather than as a poet.

What do you make of Duncan's following Olson back to Black Mountain?

Don't get me wrong. Olson was a wonderful man, a stimulator and an engenderer. One of the truly big men of our time, mentally as well as physically. His enthusiasms were profound and contagious. In a word he had awesome charisma—"heavy karma," as the hippies used to say. But he was not a great writer, a great poet. And this seriously limited his literary theories. For a theory is only as great as the sensibility that conceived it. As Rexroth said, "Charles was deaf." The result is that "composition by field" is the most disastrous doctrine to afflict the art of poetry since the prose poem. It is the alternative formulation of a poet deficient in ear, the achievement of Duncan with the method notwithstanding.

Thus Duncan's support—a poet endowed with extraordinary ear—proved a blessing to the Olsonites. For Duncan they in turn supplied the coterie accreditation, the expert opinion necessary for elitist credibility in esoteric performance. It doesn't really matter that an old Neanderthal like me, recalling our salad days back in the forties, favors only a couple Duncan poems a decade. That is more than enough to keep his name alive in the anthologies of the future. My outrageousness cannot hurt his cause. As to the reason Duncan followed Olson back to Black Mountain, all we can go by is what he said: that it was because of the *Maximus Poems*. He further said that he had always considered himself sui generis, until he read Levertov, Creeley, and Olson. It was then he realized he was part of a group.

Did you find it strange that he didn't regard himself more a part of a San Francisco or Bay Area group?

Oh, he certainly did! But that was politics, literary politics. At the level of aesthetic affinity and intellectual discernment he stood apart, feeling rather lonely till he found the Olsonites. But like politics the world over, our movement was composed of several strains of disaffiliated, disaffected memberships who had serious differences among ourselves, but due to the wintery climate prevailing in the literary scene, found ourselves banding together against the literary establishment. The various strains can be identified via their sources. Duncan claimed Pound; Ferlinghetti claimed Reverdy; Rexroth claimed Williams; Snyder and Whalen claimed Williams also; Lamantia claimed the surrealists; I don't recall who Broughton and McClure pointed to; I claimed Jeffers. As long as we were in struggle with the academics and the publicational monopoly, we stuck together, but once we had surfaced enough to let some fresh air in, the fragmentation began.

It was Duncan's acceptance of and by the Black Mountain group that marked the turning of his career.

Yes. The San Francisco identity had been too circumscribed by local insular limitations to register effectively on the national consciousness, and the Beat explosion as it erupted in the fifties found him unresponsive to its ethos. But the Black Mountain movement escaped these limitations. Donald Allen's breakthrough anthology, *The New American Poetry* in 1960, led off with Black Mountain, Duncan in strong second place, and his success was instantaneous. His highly evolved improvisational skills enabled him to assimilate the Black Mountain aesthetic perspective in short order, and his three most celebrated books followed one another in rapid succession across the sixties: *The Opening of the Field* in 1961, *Roots and Branches* in 1964, and *Bending the Bow* in 1968. Moreover, his vehement anti–Vietnam War poems were widely applauded. Then in the seventies the San Francisco gay movement began to amass the political clout to command civic recognition for its own. As Duncan had been one of the first gay intellectuals to emerge from the closet in World War II, he soon became a widely respected local celebrity, accounting for the front page exposure in the metropolitan press on the occasion of his death. As I mentioned before, this surprised me, but apparently no one else.

Did you read Duncan's later work, Groundwork I *or* II?

Not really. I tried the first one a few times, found nothing I could get my teeth into, and put it aside. It's a good example of what I said earlier about the experimental work, which got even more so as he aged, not surprisingly.

What about the earlier poetry?

I favor his early maturity where he balanced the two sensibilities, the head and the heart. I quoted "An African Elegy." It is one of the most forceful of Duncan's achievements. Capable of work like that I wish he had never heard of Black Mountain.

You got to know Duncan through his friend and co-editor James Cooney in about 1940.

Yes. I had corresponded with Cooney, who had advertised his journal, *The Phoenix,* as being Lawrentian. When Duncan moved to Woodstock to work with Cooney, he saw my letters and wrote me that he liked my poem "Orion," which I had submitted. This started a pretty intense correspondence. I didn't meet him until about a year later. He was hitchhiking from Bakersfield to Berkeley, and he stopped by in Selma for an afternoon. We lost contact a little during the war.

Then your friendship was resumed in the Bay Area after the war.

Yes. Mary Fabilli, whom I would marry, had been a friend of Robert's for many years. Earlier he had given me a print she had done, which I had hanging on my wall for a good number of years before I met her. When Mary and I got together, it brought me closer into Robert's circle, though I always felt he was a little threatened by our relationship. It was at this point, about 1947 or '48, that I began to become aware of certain competitive strains between Robert and me that hadn't been there before. We were at our closest during that period. Mary would invite him over for dinner fairly often. Sometimes the situation was a little strained. Mary had moved out of her bohemian phase and was finding him hard to take at times; when he became hysterically entertaining and outrageous, and deliberately so, she would suffer a bit, so that I couldn't enjoy it either.

Did he show you much work during this time?

Our relationship was mainly social, though he showed me a few things. The aesthetic dimension was taken up by the soiree readings around Berkeley. I've always admired Robert as a poet, even though I can't understand a lot of his poetry. I think that his homosexuality and his problem with his vision are the two things that enabled him to handle the modernist technique with such authority. These gave him an orientation that normal people don't have.

So he would necessarily carry over these aspects of his daily life into the life of his writing.

Yes. This takes us back to his concentration on accidentals. He grew up looking between two things. One eye focused one place, one another, which made him constantly aware of the correspondence between two things. This correspondence became the field wherein he wrote. It became the relevant area so that his whole vocabulary, his whole intonation, his style, were all oriented around the visionary duality. One problem with the tangible is that it becomes banal all too soon, and it is this banality that the modernist seeks to avoid at all costs. He keeps his subject matter low profile and his affect high.

When you use the term tangible *what exactly do you mean?*

The concreteness of subject matter.

In your article on Duncan in Credences *you mention a few reservations about his work.*

I think my reservations are more cogent than my acceptances. I thirst for substances and Robert doesn't press the thrust through to the consequence. I'm an incarnationist and I'm often frustrated by his poems. Even in the best work, which is some of the best our age has produced, I want to see him press further into the archetype. When he rounds a poem out it's because for that particular project he's arrived at a satisfactory equation between being and nonbeing.

Can you think of a particular example of this?

Well, take a poem like "Persephone." That was a very early poem, one that Robert sent me in an early letter. I was always impressed with his capacity to go for broke sexually; he had the forthrightness to be explicit, which very few people did in those days. I was the same, only from a heterosexual standpoint. We fought the critics off back to back. In "Persephone" he has that wonderful phrase, "Spore-spotted Onan, baldheaded, trickling with seed,/ moved among us . . ." It's so graphic that it sends me. But then he goes off into intangibles again. You can't let an insight like that just go by the board. You have to make something of it.

What do you think of the Ekbert Faas biography, Young Robert Duncan?

Terrific. I thought I knew Robert, but I found I hardly knew the first thing about him. His incredible early life carries the account. You find yourself marvelling that he survived at all, then that he emerged with intelligence intact. Some of my friends were put off by the fact that English is not Faas's first language, but in my reading that proved a plus. The Europeans bring a more historical and objective biographical perspective to the individual life, which effects a kind of cultural canonization that Robert's heroic courage, intrepid eccentricity, and aesthetic integrity can sustain. The stiff, rather formal diction, detachedly unshockable, puts its painful burden in benign perspective. I predict the book will prove to be one of the cardinal elements in Duncan's posthumous literary reputation.

How did Duncan regard it?

When I finished reading it I sat down and wrote Robert a letter intensely reaffirming all our friendship had meant to me.

He told me later that the letter arrived at a decisive moment for him. The book itself had depressed him (as well it might), and he tended to fault the author for that. But after my letter he took heart, and I know that in his next reading at Davis he brought the book along for sale with his poetry texts. I rank it among the top two or three literary biographies I have read.

Faas devotes much of his narrative to Duncan's homosexuality. Do you feel his homosexuality influenced his work beyond its specific subject matter and imagery?

Absolutely. The Apollonian tension in the work comes directly out of his homosexuality. I used to regard him as a Dionysian because of the dithyrambic sensibility, yet he points to the prophetic side of Apollo as his archetype, at least in conversation with me. He formalizes his homosexuality through the Apollonian/Dionysian equation, identifying with Apollo and rejecting Dionysus. This is the basis of his work.

When did you discover he was gay?

It was implicit in the work he sent and confirmed when he was living with Hamilton and Mary Tyler in Berkeley in the 1940s. They were good friends of mine. Either they told me, or maybe it was George Leite, editor of *Circle*.

Did this change your attitude towards him?

I recognized it as soon as I met him, but interestingly I never let it interfere with our friendship. For some reason it didn't threaten me. His disposition is so generous that my masculinity didn't feel threatened. I never needed to make any kind of adjustment. Whoa! Wait a minute. I just remembered he made a pass at me once. It was right after my release as a conscientious objector. He knew that my marriage was on the rocks and that I was grasping at straws. Woman straws, of course! I was staying a few days with Lee Watkins in Berkeley, before heading for Sonoma and the Tylers. Robert dropped by one afternoon with a poem he was writing. We discussed it at length. The next morning he showed up unannounced and handed me a note. It contained maybe three or four lines of explicit fellatio, and I protested, "Robert, it's too explicit! It will overbear the poem. You've got to come up with something less sensational!" He took the note back and left without saying a word. I then realized it was a pass. Nothing like that ever happened again, but we did have a strange and intense relationship at times.

Meaning?

As I explained in my *Talking Poetry* interview, for example, when I gave a reading at the Bancroft (or rather at Wheeler Hall *for* the Bancroft) to celebrate their acquisition of my archive, Duncan was in the audience with two young gay poets. I got a standing ovation, but Robert who was sitting just ahead of me four or five rows back, had been put off by James Hart's introduction, which he more or less laughed through. As everyone rose to their feet, Robert declined to stand. I understood this, though I was hurt by it. That was probably the hardest day in our forty-year friendship.

What did you make of his decision not to publish for fifteen years?

I thought it was suicide, but it turned out that he knew what he was doing. He emerged from that silence increased in prestige and in purpose.

When was the last time you saw Duncan?

Three years ago. He came down here with our mutual friend Al Gelpi to spend the afternoon. He had already undergone treatment for his kidney problem and had his portable dialysis machine with him. He had never been here before. We really didn't talk about anything consequential, but it was a good and healing visit. Actually, the healing had come several years earlier, at a conference on the San Francisco Renaissance at U.C. San Diego. It was a good conference, with lively exchange during the day sessions, and the night readings well attended by the public—though with the inevitable ego trips and partisan rhetoric. On my night to ready my Parkinson affliction was acting up, and I just stood at the lectern to cover my shaking; I read for an hour, just a straight reading with no pyrotechnics. When I had finished, Duncan came up, his face glowing, his crossed eye shining, and said in hushed tones, "My God, Bill, you cut through all the shit!" I am blessed in my life to have had the friendship of a great man.

In closing can you speak of Duncan's death, how you saw it in terms of his life?

Apparently he died utterly at peace, in the arms of his housemate and longtime companion, Jess Collins, a very edifying death, given the sensationalism of his early years. I think of him as protected by his Muse, living through the great San Francisco Aids epidemic of the 1980s, untouched by it all. Actually, beauty as a property of divinity is an ancient philosophical tenet of both the East and West traditions, and in our time Nicholas Berdyaev, the great Russian existentialist thinker, made a strong case for the sanctity of the great artist. When I think of Duncan's invincible courage, aesthetic integrity, and purity of vision, the dross falls away and I experience him again in his essential being, his beautiful soul confirmed in the poet's own degree of sainthood.

4 ❀ "The Sun Is But a Morning Star": Notes on Gary Snyder

1. Han-shan and the Question of Translation

> "An art of shadows and echos."
>
> —*Octavio Paz*

Kenneth Rexroth, whose fourteen books of translations include many poems from the Chinese, argued in a symposium on "Chinese Poetry and the American Imagination" (*Ironwood*, 1981) that Chinese poetry probably began to influence a few English-speaking writers when *Three Hundred Poems of T'ang* was translated into French free verse in the mid-nineteenth century. Certainly the English translations of eary sinologist Herbert A. Giles, collected in his *Gems of Chinese Literature,* marked in their archaic and doggerel renderings no advance in verse; Giles's short reworking of Wei Ying-Wu's "Spring Joys":

> When freshlets cease in early spring
>   and the river dwindles low,
> I take my staff and wander
>   by the banks where the wild flowers grow.
> I watch the willow-catkins
>   wildly whirled on every side;
> I watch the falling peach-bloom
>   lightly floating down the tide.

Nonreaders of French, Rexroth continues, of course had to wait until the turn of the century for first Arthur Waley's translations, then Ezra Pound's (and he finds the work of both Waley and Pound in this area lacking, as it gives the appearance that Chinese poetry is "as dependent on quantitative rhythms as on accentual"). Still, the effect of Chinese poetry (and Fenellosa's theoretical grounding "The Chinese Written Character as a Medium for Poetry") on verse in English was of course profound, entering the "American and to a much less degree, English poetic consciousness at exactly the right moment to purge the rhetoric and moralizing of 19th Century Romantic poetry and even more moralistic preachy poetry of the 90's." Pretty much across the board—from Imagism to Objectivism, from H.D. to Oppen—its influence was felt.

Rexroth finds the work of Waley lacking, yet, Robert Duncan: "The person who is straight-line Rexroth is Gary Snyder. He had the same bookshelf. Both thought that Arthur Waley was a prime Chinese translator" (*Conjunctions*).

The notion of a poet translating goes back at least to Dryden, and in our century most of our more lively writers—from E.P. to Robert Bly, W. S. Merwin, and Clayton Eshleman—have taken the task of translation to be a central factor in their poetics. Rexroth was perhaps our most prolific poet-translator, working from Japanese and Chinese, as well as from the Greek anthology, Pierre Reverdy, O. V. de L. Milosz, and scattered French writers. His lecture "The Poet as Translator" (*Assays*) outlines his sense of translation as "one of the most extreme examples of special pleading." The "ideal translator" is "not engaged in matching the words of a text with the words of his own language. He is hardly even a proxy, but rather an all-out advocate."

The question of "accurate translation," for Rexroth, doesn't seem to mean, necessarily, "literal translation," but rather "imitations" in Robert Lowell's sense—"to keep something of the fire and the finish" of the originals. E. P.'s *Cathay* and "The Seafarer" really established the modern idea of translation—or one sense of it—for American poets, that is the privileging of sense or tone over absolute literal accuracy. If the translator proceeds as a scientist, Ben Belitt argues, if "a simplistic semantics and a misguided analogy with the scientific method" lead him "to identify the truth of a poem substantially with its 'words' and its 'intent,'" he will end up with a "science fiction of translation." Rather, he must give a "pulse to his language," must "make a poet's demands on the emerging English rather than a pedant's or a proctor's in some Intermediate Original" (*Adam's Dream*). The point is that when a literal translation has been accomplished, the translator's real work then begins.

Octavio Paz: "The literal is not a translation. Even in prose. Only mathematics and logic can be translated in a literal sense. Real prose—fiction, history—has rhythms and many physical properties like poetry. When we translate it, we accomplish the same as we do with poems: transformations, metaphors" (*Poet's Other Voice*).

(Eshleman: "Curiously enough, it seems as if most translators of poetry feel that there is a kind of poetry involved in making their own alterations in the original, as opposed to trying to get the original across in the second language with as much integrity to its own intentions as possible. . . . [Unlike Belitt] I'm not working my poetic fate out on Neruda's back. . . . You are reading my version of a poem which comes as close to the original text as possible" [*Talking Poetry*].)

In his essays, Rexroth argues that while "the text is always in control," the greatest translators of Chinese (Judith Gautier,

Klabund, E.P.) "knew less than nothing of Chinese when they did their best translations." Witter Bynner's translation of Yuan Chen's "An Elegy" is, he feels, "one of the best American poems of this century" because "it conveys an overwhelming sense of identification with the situation of the original author. Mistakes, or at least dubious interpretations of a few words, have been pointed out since it was made, and Bynner has discarded all the obliquity and literary references of the original" ("Poet as Translator").

(*Overwhelming sense of identification*. Belitt: "I stumbled on translation simply in the process of trying to find something that was cognate with my experience of having thought about a poet, read him word for word and word by word" [*Poet's Other Voice*].)

For Rexroth, where sinologists are "too close to the language as such and too fascinated by its special very unEnglish and yet curiously English-like problems ever to see text as literature," poets, even if for all intents and purposes comparatively illiterate in the language from which they are working, can convey the proper "sympathy." (Eshleman: "I'm very much against the situation of the poet who doesn't know the language he's translating from going to a native speaker, getting literal versions of the poems, then 'poeticizing' them. Anything can happen there." James Laughlin, Rexroth's friend and publisher, says that he discovered "the source of his first Japanese and Chinese translations, rather to his chagrin. I was poking around in his library one day and I came on some French translations of the oriental poets done in the 1890's, which seemed very familiar. I read them against Kenneth's translations and discovered that he had drawn them from the French of Judith Gautier. Nothing wrong with that. Later he taught himself many Chinese and Japanese characters and worked directly" [*American Poetry*, 1984].)

Now [Rexroth] the poet recognizes this "sympathy, or projection, can carry you too far," as in the case of the French reaction to translations of Poe: "nobody in France seems to be able to learn ever that Poe's verse is dreadful doggerel and his ratiocinative fiction absurd and his aesthetics the standard lugubrations that go over in Young Ladies Study Circles and on the Chautauqua Circuit." Sympathetic translations can often hide the warts of the original. (Eshleman: "You want to show the poet in his weaknesses and strengths, in his dullness and his great moments.") Yet, from the poet's viewpoint, translation "can provide us with poetic exercise on the highest level," it can keep poets' "tools sharp," and most important "the writer who can project himself into the exultation of another learns more than the craft of words. He learns the stuff of poetry. It is not just his prosody he keeps alert, it is his heart" "Poet As Translator".)

Actually, Rexroth's "chagrin" in the face of Laughlin's discovery aside, he tends to be quite open as to his method and aim. His introduction to *One Hundred Poems from the Chinese* (1971) admits that the first part of the book—thirty-five poems by Tu-Fu—takes "note of William Hung's prose translations, of Florence Ayscough's literal renderings, and of the German of Erwin von Zach"; he describes some of the translations as being "very free," others as being "as exact as possible." The second part of the book—an anthology of Sung Dynasty poetry—includes work where at times, he says frankly, he didn't even have a Chinese text available, but rather worked from, usually, French translations: "Later I took my translations to the originals and changed them around to suit myself . . . more often freer. . . . I hope in all cases they are true to the spirit of the originals, and valid English poems." (Eshleman: "The 'spirit of the text' is a nice phrase, but the spirit of the text ends you up, I'm afraid, in

iron–clad trousers.") He even goes so far in his translations as to
"'translate out' or paraphrase many Chinese historical and literary references."

Why *Asian* poetry beyond prosodaic influence? As Rexroth
writes in "The Influence of Classical Japanese Poetry on Modern American Poetry" (*World Outside the Window*), Japanese poetry could help overcome Western alienation, as "classic Japanese culture provided those nutriments for which the West was
starved," nutriments which in "the Far East are usually connected with reactionary politics," but to us seem "about as
radical politically as they could well be." Further, Rexroth's
own poetry returns again and again to the problems of love,
loneliness, and relationship with nature, all standard themes in
classical Chinese and Japanese literature, as in one of his later
translations from Wang Yu Ch'en (with Ling Chung), "Boat-
ing on Wu Sung River":

> The setting sun leaks through the sparse,
> Slender, flowering rushes.
> For half a day I've been alone
> Chanting poems
> And haven't crossed the river.
> Only the egrets have understood me.
> Time after time they come
> Stand on one leg and look in the boat window.

Certainly, also, there was a great identification with the landscape. Gary Snyder ("East West Interview," 1977) dates his
own interest in Chinese art from about the time he was "eleven
or twelve": "I went into the Chinese room at the Seattle art
museum and saw Chinese landscape paintings; they blew my
mind. My shock of recognition was very simple: 'It looks just
like the Cascades.' The waterfalls, the pines, the clouds, the

mist looked a lot like the northwest United States. The Chinese had an eye for the world that I saw as real. In the next room were the English and European landscapes, and they meant nothing. It was no great lesson except for an instantaneous deep respect for something in Chinese culture that always stuck in my mind and that I would come back to again years later."

Years later, he did. While an undergraduate anthropology major at Reed College, Snyder discovered both Waley's and Pound's translations, Confucius, the *Tao Te Ching* (Rexroth: "Arthur Waley, whose translation is still by far the best," *Elastic Retort*), and many works of Chinese and Indian Buddhist literature. While Snyder admits that he valued Pound highly "as a teacher in poetic technology" (this influence can be seen most readily in *Myths & Texts*), his own interest in Chinese poetry came as much from inspiration of the figure of the Chinese "hermit poet / nature poet" as from an interest in technique.

Snyder's first "collection" of poems to see print actually appeared a year before *Riprap,* when in 1958 in its sixth issue *Evergreen Review* published his translations from the seventh-century Chinese poet Han-shan, along with a short introduction and a few notes on the text. (In 1965, Four Seasons Foundation would publish an edition with *Riprap;* 1970, Press-22 a limited holograph edition, lettered by Michael McPherson.)

Snyder discovered Han-shan while doing graduate work in the Department of the Oriental Languages at Berkeley in the fall of 1955. He had been taking seminars in Chinese poetry and had done a few translations of T'ang poems, when his interest in Buddhism in particular prompted him to ask Professor Ch'en Shih-hsiang to direct him in a tutorial on a Chinese Buddhist poet. Dr. Shin-hsiang suggested Han-shan, whose work at that time had been rendered into English only sparsely

(Waley's "27 Poems by Han-shan" had appeared in *Encounter* in 1954. Burton Watson's *Cold Mountain: 100 Poems by the T'ang Poet Han-shan* appeared in 1962.)

Of Dr. Shin-hsiang, Snyder told me during an interview at his house just outside Nevada City in the foothills of the Sierras in 1974, he was "not a Buddhist, as indeed all contemporary Chinese intellectuals are not Buddhist, and I think he had a certain amount of anti-Buddhist feeling as all contemporary Chinese do." But, he noted, the Han-shan project changed his mind a bit, "partly in seeing the excitement with which I put it into English; it made him see the possible freshness in it as before he had seen it as a kind of stale set of ideas."

Han-shan. We know almost nothing of his life, save that he was a reclusive poet who lived during the T'ang Dynasty (seventh-century A.D.). Lu-ch'iu Yin, an official of the dynasty, wrote a short preface to Han-shan's three hundred-plus poems, in which he explained that he caught sight of the poet (and his friend Shih-te) only once. Watson's preface: "I saw two men standing in front of the stove warming themselves and laughing loudly. I bowed to them, whereupon the two raised their voices in chorus and began to hoot at me. They joined hands and, shrieking with laughter, called out to me, 'Blabbermouth, blabbermouth Feng-kan! You wouldn't know the Buddha Amitabha if you saw him! What do you mean by bowing to us?' And the two strange men ran off and disappeared into the mountains."

(Writing this last line, oddly, I remember making our way to Snyder's in the late morning, December 8, 1974, parking some distance from his house, walking through the forest, lost. We happened upon a geodesic dome ["Geodesic domes, that / Were stuck like warts / In the woods," *Turtle Island*, 1974], blanket down across the doorway; a very lovely young woman with blond hair falling over her shoulders pulled the blanket back and, naked in the cold, directed us further down the hill where [though she didn't know the Snyders] she thought a family was building a house.)

According to Lu-ch'iu Yin, he then organized a group of monks to collect Han-shan's poems, which the poet had written on "trees and rocks or the walls of the houses and offices in the nearby village." Thus, Cold Mountain, after the vivid mountain landscape Han-shan describes. But as Waley notes, Cold Mountain is more than a place—it is also a state of mind: "It is on this conception, as well as on that of the 'hidden treasure,' the Buddha who is to be sought not somewhere outside us, but 'at home' in the heart, that the mysticism of the poem is based" (Encounter).

Snyder was certainly familiar with Waley's translations, and he was obviously drawn to Han-shan's work as both a circumstance of place and a state of mind. His short preface to his translations presents Han-shan as a kind of archetypal Beat wanderer and holy man, a "mountain man in an Old Chinese line of ragged hermits," not unlike Jack Kerouac's sense of Snyder himself in The Dharma Bums. In fact, Snyder carries the identification even further, as he feels that his own experience in the mountains of the northwest helped him capture the ethos of the originals in a way other translators could not.

(After walking his property, examining the outdoor sauna [no running water/electricity that early at his place], then through the house [built with a combination of Native American and Japanese architectures; he wanted no photograph of the house that day], he said at the kitchen table drinking wine:) "I was able to do fresh, accurate translations of Han-shan because I was able to envision Han-shan's world because I had much experience in the mountains and there are many images in Han-shan which are directly images of mountain scenery and mountain terrain and mountain weather that if a person had not felt those himself physically he would not be able to get the same feel into the translation—it would be more abstract. I think that was part of the success of those translations—a meeting of sensations."

(Earlier, while in his study, he showed me the dozen or so cardboard boxes which held all his papers—manuscripts, letters, a collection of his publications—including the pocket notebooks he kept while on secluded fire lookout for the Forest Service. *Mountain scenery and mountain terrain and mountain weather.*)

In an earlier version of this note (*Sagetrieb,* 2:1), I likened Snyder's sense of translation to Pound's / Rexroth's; that is, Lowell: "keep something equivalent to the fire and the finish of the originals" (*Imitations*). In part this was because of a letter to the linguist Dell Hymes in which Snyder explains his method of translation with explicit reference to his versions from the Chinese: "I get the verbal meaning into my mind as clearly as I can, but then make an enormous effort of visualization, to 'see' what the poem says, nonlinguistically, like a movie in my mind, and to feel it. If I can do this (and much of the time the poem eludes this effort) then I write the scene down in English. It is not a translation of the words, it is the same poem in a different language, allowing for the peculiar distortions of my own vision—but keeping it straight as possible. If I can do this to a poem the translation is uniformly successful, and is generally well received by scholars and critics. If I can't do this, I can still translate the words, and it may be well received, but it doesn't feel like it should" (Hymes, *American Anthropologist,* 1965).

In addition to capturing the ethos of the original, I wrote, this notion of translation also means that the English poem becomes—in its language, its imagery, and, even to an extent, its rhythm—finally as much a product of Snyder's poetic imagination as of Han-shan's. And indeed, as readers, when we study the versions of Pound, Lowell, Snyder, Bly, Kinnell, and other poets, we look to those poems to tell us as much about the interests, influences, and techniques of the translator-poets as anything else.

O. Paz: "The literal is not a translation."

While there is not quite the same sense of compression or ellipsis in Snyder's versions of Han-shan's poems as in a poem like "Praise for Sick Women," still the poems are obviously of a piece with Snyder's other early work; in fact, in 1969 he collected the early books together as *Riprap & Cold Mountain Poems,* as if to signify a unity of style and subject between his early original poems and the translations. Certainly it is difficult to detect much difference between "Mid-August on Sourdough Mountain Lookout" (the lead poem in *Riprap*) and, for example, "I settled at Cold Mountain long ago" (number seven of the sequence). The language of both poems is simple and direct, and in each we encounter a similar situation—the poet in seclusion, and his exhilaration in nature.

As an exercise, I then set one of Waley's Cold Mountain translations alongside one of Snyder's. In 1954, Waley published the following reworking of a Han-shan poem as "XVI" in his *Encounter* series:

> The people of the world when they see Han-shan
> All regard him as not in his right mind.
> His appearance, they say, is far from being attractive
> Tied up as he is in bits of tattered cloth.
> "What we say, he cannot understand;

What he says, we do not say."
You who spend all your time in coming and going,
Why not try for once coming to the Han-shan?

Snyder translated the same poem as the last in the sequence,
"24":

> When men see Han-shan
> They all say he's crazy
> And not much to look at—
> Dressed in rags and hides.
> They don't get what I say
> & I don't talk their language.
> All I can say to those I meet:
> "Try and make it to Cold Mountain."

Compared to Herbert Giles's "Spring Joys," Waley's translation is certainly less stilted: his language seems almost casual in tone. Yet beside Snyder's version, Waley's is more wordy and privileges the "poetic." Snyder has obviously tried to strip the poem to its bare essentials ("people of the world" becomes "men"; "not in his right mind" becomes "crazy"), and to give Han-shan not only a language that approximates speech, but a truly contemporary language. Where "What we say, he cannot understand; / What he says, we do not say" still retains a hint of a certain traditional poetic resonance, Snyder transforms the lines to everyman speaking: "They don't get what I say / & I don't talk their language."

Lew Welch (Meltzer, *The San Francisco Poets*): "Poi-Chui was a very great poet that used to have a peasant lady who was illiterate yet very smart. She ran a garden down the road and he would go and engage her in conversation. And then he would dump the poem on her and if she didn't recognize that he had just said a poem, he figured that he had written it right. If she had gone 'huh?' or something, if it seemed awkward to her or wrong, somehow ungraceful, then Poi-Chui would go back and fix it. He tested his stuff against a lady who had never read a poem in her life and never wanted to. That's a standard, and that's the way I feel about it." (Welch had planned to build a small cabin near Snyder's house. On May 23, 1971, he disappeared, leaving a note in his van, found by Snyder: "I had great visions but never could bring them together." Though his body was never found, it is assumed he committed suicide.)

Snyder responded to *Sagetrieb* with a brief, generally good-natured letter (21:IX:83), arguing that Lowell's "notion of translation has never satisfied me—and indeed, I do not accept Pound's 'Cathay' translations as my modern idea . . . the poems are far more literal than Bartlett realizes." He goes on to point out that he tried to "cleave to English monosyllables where possible (Chinese being monosyllabic) and eliminate articles and prepositions where I can—Chinese poetry being extremely telegraphic and terse." Most important, he argues, "People of the world becomes 'men' because the Chinese word there is *jen,* man or humankind. Same for 'crazy.'" Thus, "when we come to Bartlett's suspicion that the translation of *ch'iu ch'an* is Snyder's imagination, we find that there the Chinese actually means 'furs and wrappings' or 'hides and rags.' It is Waley who is making 'imitations'—good as he is."

If nothing else, my original article gave Snyder an opportunity to address his sense of translation explicity ("I do not accept Pound's 'Cathay' . . ."), something I do not think he had done before. Writers seldom respond to critical pieces on aspects of their work, however, and Snyder is not an exception; in fact, I have not run across a comparable public response by him to any sort of critical work before or since. So why did he choose to attempt to clarify?

Perhaps he took my piece to imply somehow that his skills in oriental languages were less than accute, which I neither intended nor, I hope, did. When he set out to translate Han-shan for his 1955 project, he had just started his serious study of Chinese and Japanese languages, and certainly could not at that point have yet gained any real fluency. Since those early courses at Berkeley, however, and following nearly a decade's work in Kyoto, Snyder's oriental language skills are obviously very accomplished. Tom Parkinson: "He is not merely interested in Buddhism but studies Japanese and Chinese so thoroughly that he is fluent in conversational Japanese and Chinese and translates easily from both languages" (*Poets, Poems, Movements*).

While Snyder may argue that his Han-shan poems are literal translations, however, that "it is Waley who is making 'imitations,'" such an assertion hardly closes the question. For example, Han-shan's originals, like most Chinese poems of his period, employ rhyme in the even-numbered lines; Snyder's English versions dispense with this rather important aspect of Han-shan's prosody. Such a strategy is, it seems to me, correct in that to retain the rhyme might well do violence to the English, yet obviously this approach makes a major compromise with any sense of the literal.

As to the lexical question, Snyder points out that "the original poems are all in 5 or 7 character lines. If my translations 'strip the poem to its bare essentials' that is because those bare essentials *are* the Chinese of it." Certainly, one of the lessons both E.P. and Snyder take from Chinese ideogrammic method (E.P.: "three or four words in exact juxtaposition are capable of radiating this energy at a very high potentiality," "Osiris") is the usefulness of parataxis (Olson: "one perception must must must MOVE, INSTANTER, ON ANOTHER!" "Projective Verse"). However, it does not follow that because the character may be paratactic it necessarily equates to an English mono-syllabic word.

(Eshleman, who primarily argues for the literal: "When Vallejo uses the word *casco*, there are immediately four or five words that are 'accurate' translations—skull, helmet, shard, hoof all come to mind. So I must pick. It is as if I had a file of density for the word facing me, and even if I'm trying to be as accurate as I can I must pick one level for that word. I must take skull, for example, or hoof, and the difference between them on a certain level is enormous. So without wanting to I have considerably reduced the density in the original Spanish and thus have performed an interpretational act on Vallejo," *Talking Poetry*.)

Snyder's own example undercuts his attempt to stress the literal: *ch'iu ch'an* (which is already a translation from character to alphabet; Paz: "In poetry you cannot separate the sign from the meaning"), he says "means 'furs and wrappings' *or* 'hides and rags.'" Furs and hides are not, of course, synonymous; neither are wrappings and rags. In his translation he chooses, from his "file of density," the latter. The point of my argument was the importance of that choice not in terms of reading *Han-shan* per se, but rather as an act of reading *Snyder's* reading of an earlier text. In other words, any aspect of translation—from choosing a text to choosing a word—is, as Eshleman admits, an "interpretational act," and it is the broader meaning of that act in terms of the poet-translator's own poetics which is of primary interest. If you really want to read Han-shan (or Homer, or Paz), it has always seemed to me, you obviously should go to the original rather than work through a filter. Yet if your interest is Rexroth, say, or E.P., or Snyder, or Merwin, their renderings into American of foreign texts are both integral to the larger bodies of their work as well as vivid indices to their own methodologies and thematic concerns. Looked at from this perspective, Snyder's facility in Chinese becomes largely irrelevant.

"If the translator does not feel while he reads, and simply gives a series of rhythmless dictionary meanings, he may think he is being 'faithful,' but in fact he is totally misrepresenting the original" (Waley, "Notes on Translation," 1958).

In his note Snyder closes with the comment that "finally, the rhythms of the translations, then, reflect the Chinese line, and are not part of a personal poetic strategy." The question, however, is not one of imputing Snyder or Rexroth or E.P. with a kind of literary imperialism. Rather, it is an attempt to point out the fact that Snyder is drawn to Han-shan precisely *because of* his personal poetic strategy, both in its specifics and in a broader sense. When he reads Han-shan he *feels* in a way that when he reads Baudelaire, for example, he does not:

> I've lived at Cold Mountain—how many autumns.
> Alone, I hum a song—utterly without regret.
> Hungry, I eat one grain of immortal-medicine
> Mind solid and sharp; leaning on a stone.

2. Myths & Texts *and the Monomyth*

It has been almost thirty years since Snyder's long poem *Myths & Texts* was published entire by Totem Press, yet aside from a few contemporary reviews, the poem has aroused little critical comment.[1] Even disregarding Ezra Pound's thirty-year "time lag," the lack of sustained critical treatment of *Myths & Texts* is not really surprising. While the poem usually remained in print through its original small-press publisher, until recently it had never been collected in any of the poet's more readily available New Directions volumes.[2] Further, many critics still look upon writers identified with the Beat Generation (Snyder was the model for Japhy Ryder in Jack Kerouac's *Dharma Bums*) with some ill ease, and the poem itself is the product of a fairly labyrinthine Asian and Native American mytho-poetics.

Though the poem's method is modernist (fragmentary rather than narrative), and the verse is Poundian in its refinement of the image, the thematic movement is decidedly romantic as it traces the overthrow of the Apollonian tendencies towards culture, education, and the ego by the Dionysian impulses toward the primitive, ecstasy, and the unconscious. The romantic, as Morse Peckham notes, can be identified in part by her threefold movement: confrontation of the Void, subsequent psychic disorientation and search for renewal, and final transcendence through the discovery of new ways of locating value in the self through a (re)integration with the natural world. Joseph Campell describes this movement as the "monomyth": separation—initiation—return.[3] The three principle divisions of *Myth & Texts,* "Logging," "Hunting," and "Burning," mirror this archetypal monomyth. They assert both the physical and psychic dislocations of the narrator from the life-denying, Apollonian impulses of his culture, his quest for an alternative to that negation, and the final realization of a new vision born out of the flames of a dying civilization.

Section 1, "Logging," which takes much of its imagery from Snyder's experiences as a logger in Oregon, presents a modern wasteland produced through an Apollonian desire to control the forces of nature. "Logging I," which opens with a reference to the last sentence of *Walden,* "the sun is but a morning star," establishes the theme of the poem as the possibility for regeneration emerges from a dream-vision of Dionysian ecstasy. Images of fertility abound. The invocation is to Io, the wandering moon-cow aspect of the Great Mother, who in Egyptian mythology was worshiped as Isis, the regenerative force returning life to Horus after he was stung by a scorpion. It is the rutting season, and while the Pleiades circle the Maypole, birds are active and "green comes out of the ground." Young girls carrying thyrsus are overwhelmed by Dionysian frenzy, as all nature seems to erupt in orgiastic fertility rites.

"Logging 2" shocks us into consciousness, as the narrator—Snyder—awakens from his dream of May Queens and maenads to the stark, cold world of the logger. Here we get our first vision of a land laid waste by men in "tin pisspot hats" driving "crummy trucks" and "Cats," a vision which will be developed throughout this section. In praise of an ordered and reasonable civilization, the forests of both China and Seattle have been logged. In the wreckage, only the lodgepole pine, which has the ability to "endure a fire / which kills the tree without injuring its seed" (I, 3), presents a chance for regeneration out of the 250,000 board feet a day of future 2 × 4s moved out by the loggers. Philosophy and religion, "the ancient, meaningless / abstractions of the educated mind" (I, 5), are useless against this destruction, for they have their source in the Apollonian. Neither is classical literature a help, as Seami Motokiyo and Kwanami, masters of the Nō, have disappeared into the pines.[4] The berries which were plentiful just a few hours before are gone, workers are degraded and even shot "for wanting a good bed, good pay, / decent food, in the woods" (I, 7), and the destruction goes on. Tractors smash boulders and grass, trees fall, and bees "circle above the crushed dead log, their home," until all that is left are "a few stumps, drying piles of brush" (I, 8).

The job completed, Snyder hitchhikes to meet his girl for a weekend of love-making, talk, and bathing. While he is in town, a "ghost logger" in "Sagged pants" (I, 10) happens upon the deserted logging camp. Like the temple of the goddess

Diana at Nemi, the camp is in ruins, settled between rotting stumps. The Christian (patriarchal) emanation of the Apollonian impulse has succeeded in pulling down the forests, but what was it all for? The logger is old, flea-bitten, broke, and the wood he has cut has long outlived its usefulness.

As the apocalyptic vision draws to a close, Snyder and another logger named Ray Wells make a symbolic blood sacrifice to the Apollonian, as they discuss the gelding of ponies (a suggestion of sterility juxtaposed to the images of regeneration and fertility introduced in "Logging 1"). As the forests continue to fall to the Cats, Drinkswater, an Oglala Sioux shaman, sees the life to come in a land once inhabited by salmon, bear, wild ducks, and oysters: "You shall live in square / gray houses in a barren land / and beside those square gray houses you shall starve" (I, 12). The last forests are burning, "turning the late sun red / . . . smoke filling the west" (I, 13), and the logging crews depart. Snyder, who has up to this point taken part in the destruction, is left alone to contemplate the void of the waste land. As the patriarch Jehovah commanded in the opening of "Logging 2," the groves of Ahab and of Cybele, the Phrygian Great Mother, have been

> Cut down by the prophets of Israel
>   the fairies of Athens
>   the thugs of Rome
>   both ancient and modern;
> Cut down to make room for the suburbs
> Bulldozed by Luther and Weyerhaeuser
> Crosscut and chainsaw
>   squareheads and finns
>   high-lead and cat-skidding
> Trees choked, trout killed, roads.
> Sawmill temples of Jehovah

> Squat black burners 100 feet high
> Sending the smoke of our burnt
> Live sap and leaf
> To his eager nose.

(I, 14)

The Apollonian destruction has left nothing in its wake, save the single lodgepole pine whose "cone / seed waits for fire" (I, 15). It is the end of the kalpa (in Hindu mythology an age consisting of a night and a day of Brahman, or 8,640,000,000 years), and like the painter Pa-ta Shan-jen who witnessed the fall of the Ming Empire, Snyder must realize that his world of "men who hire men to cut groves, / kill snakes, build cities, pave fields, / believe in god but can't / believe in their own senses" (I, 15) has come to a close.

As its title "Hunting" implies, the second section of *Myths & Texts* traces a search through a variety of primitive traditions and mythologies for a new vision, a regenerative one; it is the second step of Campbell's monomyth, initiation. "Hunting" begins with the "first shaman song," which is appropriate as the shaman (maker of the dance) is both the first artistically creative man known to us and the archetypal Dionysian figure. As the section opens, Snyder is sitting in the "village of the dead," surrounded by evidence of the loggers' destruction: loose bones, smoking grass, logs floating aimlessly in the river. He has gone thus far two days without food—the start of his symbolic purification—and now, as the last truck pulls away, he sits quietly without thinking, his unconscious "hatching a new myth" to sustain him.

We are introduced to hunters of various sorts (II, 2), indicating that the need for regeneration has been an ongoing historical process in both Eastern and Western cultures. As Snyder begins his vision-quest, his search for renewal, we have a sense that his answer lies somewhere in the natural world; the sky is suddenly full of birds whose patterns define the future if he can only learn to read them. A storm is approaching (the quest will be neither an easy nor a pleasant one), but it cannot be avoided, for as the Vaux swifts cry, he must "see or go blind" (II, 3). Again, the necessity for engaging nature directly is stressed ("brushed by the hawk's wing / of vision"), as is the confusion caused by the Apollonian need to define and classify:

> —They were arguing about the noise
> Made by the Golden-eye Duck.
> Some said the whistling sound
> Was made by its nose, some said
> No, by the wings.
>   "Have it your own way.
> We will leave you forever."
>
>   (II,4)

According to Snyder, the sources for "this poem is for bear" (II, 6) are in Marius Barbeau's Bella-Coola collections, an article by A. O. Hallowell on the "circumpolar Bear Cult," and his "own encounters with Bears."[5] In this crucial passage, a girl encounters Bear (like Snyder, the archetypal Wanderer, "Odysseus was a bear"), by whom she has decidedly Dionysian children ("slick dark children / with sharp teeth"). The girl's brothers discover her marriage—an attempt at fusing the human with the natural—chase her "husband," and kill him. Nature rebels at this wanton destruction as all the small headwater streams dry up. The passage ends with Snyder suggesting he'll go hunt bears, a Faulknerian coming of age; he isn't yet ready for the knowledge, however, as his initiation is not complete: "Why shit Snyder, / you couldn't hit a bear in the ass / with a handful of rice."

In II, 7, both the cyclic essence of reality and the necessity for an organic unity are again stressed. Dawn reveals rabbits hanging from snares, but as their capture is according to a natural cycle rather than mindless destruction (i.e., the Shuswap tribe is going to use them for food), their deaths are first pastoral, then celebrative, as they sing of their reincarnation. Unlike the loggers, the Shuswap are in tune with their environment; they live on salmon, deer, roots, and berries, while they eschew pottery (symbolic of the technology which separates man from nature); their houses are constructed according to the seasons; like the girl and the bear of the previous section, the village girls "get layed by Coyote," but because there is a strong link to the natural, this causes no strife: "We get along just fine."

"This poem is for deer" (II, 8) is the longest passage in "Hunting," and probably its locus, as here Snyder confronts his own guilt for siding with Apollonian destructiveness. At the start, the sense of alienation from the natural world is reiterated as hunters, after missing a shot at a deer, run to their automobiles through an unfriendly forest ("we came back sliding / on dry needles through cold pines"). A rabbit appears and for no real reason one of the hunters shoots off its head; where in the previous passage the death of rabbits is celebrated by even the rabbits themselves as simply a stage in the Great Wheel, here the death becomes grotesque (though "realistic") as "the white body rolls and twitches / in the dark ravine" of the Apollonian. This act invokes a sort of primal scream from a deer on the mountain (probably the one they had just attempted to kill), setting it "howling like a wise man." Later, the hunters catch a "four-point buck / dancing in the headlights," and they shoot the "wild silly blinded creature down." In the cold night they ritually disembowel the deer (not unlike the gelding of ponies in I, 11), then toss it in their trunk. But the "warm blood / . . . deer-smell, / the limp tongue" disturb Snyder in a sudden and profound way, as he realizes he has committed a crime on the order of the Ancient Mariner's shooting of the Albatross. Here he begins his final ascent into the void, the last leg of his initiation / quest, his final purification and expiation: "I'll drink sea-water / sleep on beach pebbles in the rain / until the deer come down to die / in pity for my pain." This purification is followed by the stirrings of a painful birth. Salmons mate, their "big seeds / groping for inland womb," and Snyder seems almost to rise out of them in Darwinian fashion as he becomes "a frozen addled egg on the tundra." His final salvation is full immersion into Dionysian frenzy ("I ate the spawned-out salmon / I went crazy / covered with ashes / gnawing the girls' breasts"), as he attempts a total, though violent, reintegration into the natural order ("marrying women to whales / for dogs"). As an ecstatic "priest" of this new order, he will rape the wives of the old, not simply as a violation but to infuse them with seeds of the new. An entire universe is created in a flash ("flung from demonic wombs / off to some new birth / a million shapes / . . . scattered all through the galaxy," II, 10), as Snyder calls on Prajapati, the Buddha as Creator. The initiation draws to a close as Snyder has a vision of man's reintegration into the natural world:

> I wore my Raven skin
> Dogfish ran. Too many berries on the hill
> Grizzly fat and happy in the sun—
> The little women, the fern women,
> They have stopped crying now.

(II, 11)

Snyder emerges from his ritual purging after eight days in the high country without food. He comes upon a grove of wild apple trees and picks a green apple. In an inversion of the Christian myth, this act symbolizes his dependence on, and his harmony with, his surroundings; hornets swarm around him, but he is now one of them and therefore they pose no danger ("smell of the mountains still on me. / none stung"). There is a reference to the Buddha, and like the Buddha, Snyder has experienced a sort of enlightenment which sets him apart from other men. He packs his mule ("lashed with a vajra-hitch," which is identified with enlightenment), and leaving the other workers behind, heads again up the mountain for his final vision. It is the "first day of the world," as he sees the landscape truly for the first time. Like Maudgalyâyana, Snyder has passed through hell to surface regenerated (II, 15). Part II ends with the birth of a baby, one to whom all nature reacts in a nurturing way ("Chipmunks, gray squirrels, and / golden-mantled ground-squirrels / brought him each a nut"). There is a Dionysian celebration of the birth wherein man and nature are fused: "Girls would have in their arms / a wild gazelle or wild wolf-cubs / and give them their white milk." They are wearing the skins of fawns, and are drunk on wine/truth. Both man and animal have the Buddha nature, "Meaning: Compassion."

According to Campbell's schema, in the third stage of the mono-myth the hero begins the process of his return, bringing "the runes of wisdom, the Golden Fleece, or his sleeping princess back into the kingdom of humanity, where the boon may redound to the renewing of the community, the nation, the planet, or ten thousand worlds."[6] Campbell goes on to explain that the hero often questions his charge, however, and that even the "Buddha, after his triumph, doubted whether the message of realization would be communicated." In Part III of *Myths & Texts*, "Burning," Snyder enters this stage as he attempts to come to a full reintegration with the natural world and therefore close the circle of the monomyth.

"Burning" opens with Snyder's emergence from his vision-quest:

> Crouched in a dry vain frame
> —thirst for cold snow
> —green slime of bone marrow
> Seawater fills each eye

Quivering in nerve and muscle
Hung in the pelvic cradle
Bones propped against roots
A blind flicker of nerve

Still hand moves out alone
Flowering and leafing
Turning to quartz

(III, 1)

The image is powerful, the language some of the finest in the poem. As the waters recede, Snyder moves as if out from the sea back into the world, the sun drying him as he dances his shaman's dance.

The next three sections give us "lessons," Snyder's "golden fleece." The first is that the nature of the world is in essence dualistic—an Apollonian (intellect)/Dionysian (instinct) equation—and that this dualism must be worked out in "this only world" of "juggling forms." In III, 3, we have the example of Maudgalyâyana who, like Snyder, passes through hell to a rebirth; our second lesson: we cannot escape the duality—we must "learn to love," accepting both the beauty and the horror of the world, "opening the eyes." Finally, we have a description of Maitreya, the Buddha of the next age. At first, Maitreya refuses to merge with the natural world ("stuck in a bird's craw / last night / Wildcat vomited his pattern on snow"); he shuts out sexuality and ecstasy in his refusal to dance or kiss, eats berries which leave him "bloodied," and can't cope with the notion of organic unity. But after ages of evolution (akin to Snyder's just-finished initiation), ages of "fish scale, shale dust, bone / of hawk and marmot, / caught leaves in ice," his essence is "flung on a new net of atoms," leaving his "empty happy body / swarming in the light" of enlightenment. Snyder has, in fact, become the Maitreya himself, bringing with him on his return news of the new age.

The poem continues with a series of passages wherein images of the mergence of the "human" with the "natural" are presented: a tree takes on the appearance of a man, civilization ("granite") crumbles as man returns to a more natural state in which "mayflies glitter for a day like Popes." In III, 7, a crucial section, we have a "new dawn," as Snyder dreams he sees the Duke of Chou (credited with the invention of the compass) which indicates he is on the right path back into the world. A woman is described in immediate physical terms (with Snyder burying his "face in the crook of her neck / felt throb of vein / smooth skin, her cool breasts / all naked"), and then suddenly is transformed into the Great Mother, "the Mother whose body is the Universe / whose breasts are Sun and Moon." She comes to symbolize Prajna (perfect wisdom), smiling quietly, secure in her knowledge. The transience of life is stressed, as is its solution—immortality through perfect understanding of man's place in nature, his feeding like all sentient and nonsentient begins at the "breast of the Mother of the Universe."

The next two passages give us a glimpse of those who have come before Snyder with a similar message: John Muir, who in a Zen-like experience while rock-climbing, discovers that as long as he attempts to *overcome* the rock his mind seems "filled with a / stifling smoke" and he risks falling, but as soon as he surrenders his ego to a "new sense," he moves with a precision with which he seems "to have / Nothing at all to do"; Wobblies ("forming the New Society / Within the shell of the Old"); figures like Bodhidharma (founder of Zen), Lenin, Hsuan Tsang, and the American Indian leaders Joseph and Crazy Horse. And yet, like Confucius, they have all failed to transform the world. Still, as the hero-figure, Snyder himself cannot abrogate his responsibility, and in III, 10, he repeats "Amitabha's Vow" that until all creatures are enlightened he will not proceed to nirvana.

(It is interesting to note the Beat images here—such notions as a "vagrancy rap," losing "a finger coupling boxcars," and "hitch-hiking.")

The following sections continue to make the poem's theme more explicit through a meditation (in the Zen sense of *zazen*) on koans. Snyder sits with his new "perceptions" in a "long-empty hall": "What is the way of non-activity?" (III, 11). It is activity itself—the "rush of water and bone"—for the physical, our bodies, cannot be denied. What is the nature of the city of the Gandharvas (a heavenly city of musicians in charge of soma[7])? It is the perfect organic harmony of all things, the interpenetration—a "city crowded with books" yet having "thick grass on the streets," a city of spirit and substance. In its current manifestation, "civilization" (i.e. the thrust of the Apollonian) is "too coarse" to inhabit such a place; the city becomes a mirage, "the memory of a city only, / preserved in seed from the beginningless time" (III, 12), an Eden, but that to which we must aspire. The poetry itself here becomes "a riprap on the slick rock of metaphysics," making the message clear—Apollonian destruction must be put away ("set the army horses free in the mountain pastures, / set the Buffalo free on the Plain of the Peach Grove," III, 13). Snyder has returned enlightened, but in keeping with the tradition of mystical illumination, "it was nothing special / misty rain on Mt. Baker." We plead incomprehension, while in fact all that binds us to the world of illusion is our refusal "to see" the proverbial nose in front of our collective face.

In accordance with his vow—and in closing the monomyth—Snyder comes down from his mountain into the world:

> Snow-flake and salmon,
> The pure, sweet, straight-splitting
>   with a ping

> Red cedar of the thick coast valleys
> Shake-blanks on the mashed ferns
>   the charred logs
>
>   (III, 15)

Like a wandering monk he travels down from the north through Sacramento, "riding flatcars to Fresno / across the whole country," watching "this whole spinning show." On the surface of the earth little has changed as the fires have left smoke, "soot and hot ashes" for a thousand miles, yet "the hot seeds steam underground / still alive" intimating the possibility of regeneration. The poem proper closes with a warning from Coyote to mankind: we must realize both the eternal circle of things and our interdependence with the natural world to achieve a transformation of consciousness.

Section 17 of "Burning" functions as a sort of envoy, making clear for us the implications of Coyote's warning. According to the "text" (i.e., the phenomenal world), Snyder has simply traveled up Thunder Creek to help put out a forest fire; at night the rain has come, the firefighters have slept, and now they have seen "the last glimmer of the morning stars." In the "myth," however, this simple event finds registration in the symbolic—Troy burns, dogs bark, children shriek—as our civilization burns itself out from its own Apollonian impulses. We refuse "to see," and with "black pit cold and light-year / flame tongue of the dragon / licks the sun" our brief age passes away. According to Campbell,

> Sirs, after the lapse of a hundred thousand years the
> cycle is to be renewed; this world will be destroyed;
> also the mighty ocean will dry up; and this broad
> earth, and Sumeru, the monarch of mountains, will
> be burnt up and destroyed—up to the Brahma
> world will the destruction of the world extend.
> Therefore, sirs, cultivate friendliness; cultivate com-

passion, joy, and indifference; wait on your mothers; wait on your fathers; and honor your elders among your kinsfolk.[8]

Yet, like the lodgepole pine, like the "hot seeds underground," another cycle will begin for (in echo of the poem's opening line) "the sun is but a morning star," heralding rebirth.

Structured on the monomyth, *Myths & Texts* follows directly in the tradition of heroic literature from the great religious texts and epics, through the romances, to romantic literature. Additionally, this early poem is Snyder's most extended treatment to date of what from *Riprap* to *Songs for Gaia* has evolved as his great theme—the affirmation of the Dionysian over the Apollonian, the call for a transformation of values and a reintegration of man and nature.

5 ❂ Meat Science to Wolf Net: Michael McClure's Poetics of Revolt

Reviewing Michael McClure's *Scratching the Beat Surface* in 1982, I wrote: In George Oppen's only review, published in *Poetry* in August of 1962 and dealing with work by Allen Ginsberg, Charles Olson, and Michael McClure, he dismisses McClure's verse as born of "excitement, intoxication, meaninglessness, a destruction of the sense of oneself among things." Assuredly, McClure's poetry is both generated by and celebrative of those Dionysian elements the Apollonian/modernist sensibility finds offensive. In terms of politics, however, Oppen's dismissal seems curious; while he and his fellow objectivists were in the main high modernists in terms of practice, Oppen himself was a left-wing activist. Further, his own work shifted from the Pound/Williams influence in the objectivist *Discrete Series* to a more subjective poetry in the mid-fifties. But where Oppen's leftist politics are occasionally programmatic (Marxist), McClure's leftist politics are at once more diffuse and more encompassing; it is here, I think, that Oppen feels from McClure a threat which goes beyond the simply aesthetic. McClure considers himself above all a poet of revolt. A 1961 essay: "at all times revolt is the search for health and naturality"; "hysteria is a real animal process"; "revolt is a striving to a regimen that is conceived of as athletic and physical." And essentially, and probably most disturbing to Oppen, "there is no political revolt. All revolt is personal" ("Revolt").

"EACH MAN, WOMAN, CHILD / is innocent / and not responsible / for the atrocities committed by any / government . . . / THAT I AM A FLOWER DOES NOT MEAN / THAT I AM RESPONSIBLE / FOR THE AGONY OF THE ROOTS!" or "Politics are theories regarding the speculated / laws of power—their applications / have never touched men except in shapes / of repression! / NEW SOCIETY WILL BE BIOLOGICAL!" (*Poisoned Wheat*, 1965).

Like a key source, Shelley, McClure is often, even sometimes painfully, rhetorical, yet his exploration of revolt is an exploration of sound. A few years ago Robert Peters likened McClure's poetry to action painting, wherein "the energy screaming (at times) streaming (at others) is as important as any direct poetic statement." As a "mammalian communicator" (Peters's term) McClure has attempted to register the raw, animal, sexual possibilities of the howl, the grunt, the spontaneous cry: "BWAHHH MORN-DRIFT HELD IN PASSAGE / GRAHHR! GRAHHR! / GAHROOOOOOOOOOOOOOOOOOOOOOOOOOOH!! / Dreeem nooothowgeeii. Brooooooon. Grahh!" (*Ghost Tantras*, 1964). "What I am most concerned with now," he tells David Meltzer in his *San Francisco Poets* interview, "is the river within ourselves. The biological energy of ourselves as extrusions or tentacles of the universe of meat."

"In Tantrism the human body acquired an importance without precedent in India's spiritual history. The body is no longer the 'source of sufferings' but the surest and most accomplished instrument available to man for the 'conquest of death'" (Mircea Eliade, *Patanjali and Yoga*). "Poetry is a muscular principle."

Tantra (whether Buddhist or Hindu) is antispeculative, antiascetic. "Since the body represents the cosmos and all the gods, since liberation can be gained only by setting out from the body, it is important to have a body that is healthy and strong . . . liberation is pure spontaneity" (Eliade, *Yoga*). Poetry is a muscular principle. The Kid (William H. Bonney, d. 1891 at 22) charmingly seducing Jean Harlow (d. 1937 at 25) in McClure's *The Beard* (December 18, 1965, the Actor's Workshop, SF; a few days later charged in Berkeley with "lewd and dissolute conduct in a public place"): "YOU'RE A BAG OF MEAT! A white sack of soft skin and fat held in shape by a lot of bones! . . . Nobody's free of being divine!"

Tantra (*tan:* "multiply"; sanskrit: "to weave"). A sacred, ritualistic, transformative text. Tantras="Treatises on the Doctrine." Often centering on Shakti (energy), wife of Shiva (whose cosmic dance announces the apocalypse) and divine, in the form of a dialogue (The Kid and Ms. Harlow?). *Ghost Tantras,* "ghost texts." Or, perhaps, tantrums, a moving out of the intellect into the (hysterical) song of the body.

"When a man does not admit he is an animal, he is less than an animal. . . . Blake was the revolt of one man. He was not a revolutionary but a man in revolt. A creature in revolt can conceive that there is NO solution and that there will be unending construction and destruction. . . . Blake revolted with his being and maintained himself as a visionary mammal as best he might in his circumstances. His creature pride and his vision in works of poetry and painting survive as part of his body. REVOLT IS A BIOLOGICAL PROCESS" ("Blake and the Yogin,").

(Biographical: b. Marysville, Kansas, October 20, 1932; removes to San Francisco from Tuscon, 1955, with Joanna; enrolls in Duncan's SF State Poetry Workshop, participating in *Faust Foutu* reading; meets Ginsberg at a party for Auden; Six Gallery reading [October 13, 1955, with Rexroth, Ginsberg, Snyder, et al.] first public reading; first published poems: "2 For Theodore Roethke" [villanelles] *Poetry,* 1956; revived anarchist *Ark,* with James Harmon, *Ark II/Moby I;* first book, *Passage,* published by Jonathan Williams's Jargon, 1956; extended late-fifties correspondence with Olson [McClure's papers: Modern Literature Collection, Simon Fraser; Olson's papers: Olson Archive, Storrs]; first play: "The Raptors" [1957]; first play produced: "!The Feast!" [1960]; *Journal For the Protection of All Beings,* ed. with Ferlinghetti & Meltzer [1961], includes "Revolt"; 1962, joins faculty of California Colleges of Arts and Crafts, Oakland [professorship, 1977]; spontaneous novel: *The Mad Club* [1970]; role in N. Mailer's film "Beyond the Law," film script with Jim Morrison [The Doors {*of Perception*}], autoharp from Bob Dylan, writes "Mercedes Benz" [recorded by Janis Joplin]; report on trip to 1971 UN Evironmental Conference [Stockholm, with Snyder, Stewart Brand, Sterling Bunnel, and Joanna, rep. Project Jonnah] for *Rolling Stone; Josephine: The Mouse Singer* [first performance, NY, 1978], Obie Award for Best Play of the Year.)

Along with Rexroth, Olson, Snyder, and Tarn, McClure reads seriously "outside his discipline." Snyder in 1974: "One of my best friends, who's also one of my gurus in a way, stopped just short of his Ph.D. in biophysics, and now he fixes trucks. But whenever I have a really difficult question I go to him, on the scientific level. And he recommends books to me which I recommend to Michael sometimes" (Knight, *The Beat Diary*). M.'s "reading list" appended to *Scratching the Beat Surface* includes not only Blake, Duncan, Olson, Shelley, and Snyder, but: Garma C. C. Chang, *The Buddhist Teaching of Totality;*

Ernst Haeckel, *The Riddle of the Universe at the Close of the Nineteenth Century;* Harry J. Jerison, *Evolution of the Brain and Intelligence;* Ramon Margalef, *Perspectives in Ecological Theory;* Lynn Margulis, *Origin of Eukaryotic Cells;* Philip Tobias, *The Brain in Hominid Evolution;* et al. And of course Francis Crick, *Of Molecules and Men,* and Howard T. Odum, *Environment, Power, and Sociology.*

Crick and Odum, especially, are crucial sources, as is Morowitz, who tells McClure (who is reading Olson's "The Kingfishers" and thinking in terms of a "systemless system") that "the flow of energy through a system acts to organize the system," which is what—

Williams: "Therefore each speech having its own character the poetry it engenders will be peculiar to that speech also in its own intrinsic form";

Olson: "The poem itself must, at all points, be a high energy construct and, at all points, an energy discharge";

Levertov: "Form is never more than a revelation of content";

Creeley: "Nothing will fit if we assume a place for it."

Ginsberg: "Meaning Mind practiced in spontaneity invents forms in its own image & gets to Last Thoughts"— recognize in their own contexts.

Francis Harry Crick (b. 1916), biophysicist, purchased McClure's broadside "Peyote Poem" in San Francisco four years before winning the Nobel Prize for medicine in 1962 for his work on the double helix of the DNA molecule; he includes two lines, "THIS IS THE POWERFUL KNOWLEDGE / we smile with it," in *Of Molecules and Men.* (Crick contributes a short essay to the McClure symposium issue, *Margins,* 1975.) McClure: "Crick's use of those lines shows the important, yet little known reaching out from science to poetry and from poetry to science that

was part of the Beat movement. . . . In childhood I had intended to be a naturalist or biologist and he helped me keep that
consciousness vital" ("The Beat Surface" *in memoriam* Olson).

Re: Odum and the question of energy. Talking with Gary
Snyder at his in-progress house in the Sierra foothills in 1974 (he
was not yet serving as an advisor to Jerry Brown, and lived
with his wife and sons without telephone, electricity, and running water); he told me, when I asked him about his sense of
Buckminster Fuller's notion of "self-interferring patterns": "In
energy-system terms, bodies are temporary energy traps in
which energy is held briefly and can be deferred into other uses,
other eco-systems, on the path of energy from the sun to the
energy-sink in the universe. And so all living structures, and
perhaps all material structures, are various augmentations and
temporary constructions that energy takes on its way to the
heat-sink. H. T. Odum says that language is a form of energy
trap, and that particular kinds of communications which he
calls tiny energies in precise forms released at the right moment
amount to energy transfers that are much larger than their size
would indicate—which is what poems are, from an ecological
energy-systems man's point of view."

And McClure: "It is the surge of our physical energy that
carries us through—and we need no vanity about having it—it
is an inheritance. It is also the surge that organizes the system
into tribes. It spurts and it radiates. It is the energy that defines
poetry. 'The Kingfishers' is an ode to energy and of energy"
("The Shape of Energy," 1982).

(Last month George Butterick sent a long essay on "The Kingfishers" for *AP;* on the phone a few days later, "I think it's my
best piece on Olson," in a difficult voice from his library office.
I hadn't learned of his illness until very late, then yesterday a
letter from Paul Christensen, "George Butterick has died.")

as long as it was necessary for him, my guide
to look into the yellow of that longest-lasting rose

"The ideal of Yoga, the state of *jivan-mukti,* is to live in the 'eternal present,' outside of time. 'Liberated in life,' the *jivan-mukta* no longer possess a personal consciousness—that is, a consciousness nourished on its own history—but a witnessing consciousness, which is pure lucidity and spontaneity" (Eliade, *Yoga*).

"Pure lucidity and spontaneity." Wilhelm Reich (b. 1897, d. 1957 in Federal Penitentiary at Lewisburg, Pennsylvania), developed out of Freud's libido theory the concept of orgone, "life energy." Of the "beat writers," William Burroughs especially was drawn to Reich's thought and praxis, as was McClure, who told David Meltzer in 1969, "Reich came like a bolt out of heaven for me. I found the muscular contractions and armoring he speaks of to be quite clearly within my own body. I tried a Reichian analyst. There wasn't one on the West Coast. I worked through experiments, exercising, automatic writing, and a lot of good friends and luck to find the armorings and to do what I could to eliminate them. I was in a state of extraordinary biological distress when I stumbled onto his work. I found it to be a great godsend, messiah-send—if the messiah is the universe."

In *Function of the Orgasm* (1942), Reich argues that the orgasm represents a spontaneous discharge of sexual excitation, that "the involuntary bio-energetic contraction of orgasm and the complete discharge of excitation are the most important criteria for orgastic potency." As the point of orgasm is reached in sexual intercourse, a "clouding of consciousness" ("*beclouding of consciousness*"—Kerouac, "Essentials of Spontaneous Prose") occurs, which errupts into the ultimate Dionysian transportation out of the ego. Reich discovers that both male and female patients suffering from a variety of neuroses are unable fully to experience this transport, that they all retain a great degree of intellectual lucidity during orgasm. He concludes that this produces a sexual stasis in the individual, a clogging-up of sexual energy that fuels the neurosis. It is only when "full orgastic gratification took place in the immediate present" that sexual equilibrium and mental health might be restored.

W. Burroughs: "Reich advocated the use of orgone therapy as both a preventative and the best treatment for active cancer. He considered that cancer occurs when the electrical charge at the surface of the cells falls to a suffocation point" (*The Adding Machine*, 1985).

> ALL IS QUIET BUT MY SONG TO ME, YOUR SONG
> to you. This is our touching. This
> is the vast hall that we inhabit. Coiling,
> standing. Cock into rose-black meat. Tongue
> into rose meat. Come upon your breasts, Come
> upon your tongue, come in your burrow
> Cavern love snail breath strange arm line.

"Revolt is a striving to a regimen that is conceived of as athletic and physical. Its function is to uncover and keep alive the natural physical urges of our meat. Some of these processes are sex, desire for awareness, and desire for pleasure. Perhaps they are not divisible but all erotic" ("Revolt").

Hymns to St. Geryon and Other Poems (1959): Hercules killed Geryon, a human beast with three bodies and one pair of legs, to capture his oxen; Dante figures Geryon as falsehood, McClure as the instinctual/social strain: "I am the body, the animal, the poem / is a gesture of mine." (McClure opens the *Selected Poems*, 1986, with work from *St. Geryon*.)

Robert Bly (*News of the Universe*) reminds us that Cartesian dualism stands as the bulwark of the "Old Position," solidifying an earlier Augustinian view of nature as evil. "I think, therefore I am," privileging the mind (the city) over the body (nature). For poets like Lessing, Pope, and Arnold, nature becomes the Other, something either to be feared or disdained, while civilization offers salvation. Romanticism provides a general revolt, but Bly finds little use in the English Romantics who (save Blake) remain "primarily in the realm of feeling"; even Keats, Bly suggests, finds it necessary in a poem like "Ode to a Nightingale" to return to the comfort of human society at the last moment, unable to sustain himself in a "twofold consciousness." Bly turns to Nerval, Hölderlin, and Novalis as examples of poets who are willing to accept the "dark side" of nature in their praise of the unconscious—night, sexuality, woman—over against Wordsworthian idealization.

Harlow: "Then what's so great about me?—What do you want with a bag of meat?" (*The Beard*).

Bly continues by suggesting that we reconsider what "modern poetry" is. There is, he admits, a genuine tradition sourced in Corbière and LaForgue, and continuing through Eliot, Auden, and Lowell, and its essence is irony. The major tradition for Bly, however, is the Novalis/Hölderlin/Goethe line, a line whose mood "is not ironic but swift association." (McClure: "You see I didn't plan to write a stanza, saying 'now I'll tell about the time I went down to the candy shop'—instead one memory would bring another memory into being. Sometimes memories changed in the middle of a stanza, then I began to sense how one of them would light up another related memory and that memory would light up another and that one would light up another. Then a constellation of those three, having been lit, would light up another one which would be seemingly disparate but was related to the constellation of the three" [1974, *The Beat Journey*]). Where Eliot accepts with resignation that the mermaids will not sing to him, poets of the primary tradition (Rilke, Lawrence, Snyder, McClure) will not, as they refuse to collapse into a Cartesian dualism.

1961: "Body is the major force, and intellect is a contained auxiliary. . . . The physiological processes of the Body, and the emotions, desires, hungers, organs, nerves, etc. are the Body. And the Body, as in the planaria, *is* Spirit. . . . There is a single SELF now, I know it and feel it" ("Revolt"). *1982:* "It is our overabstracted nature that does not see the complexity, or feel the complexity, of the body. Charles Olson realized that when he wrote his essay, 'Projective Verse'. . . . There is no separation between body and mind" ("The Shape of Energy").

Ghost Tantras, beast language. The Fall is, perhaps, a fall into language. It is language, words (the mind—"I think, therefore I am"), which forces us into dualistic thinking, as each word represents a conceptual category. The more literate we are, the more "civilized," the further we are from the Garden, from the body. (Thus women, constantly reminding men of their corporeal selves, in all patriarchal religions—from mainline Christianity to conservative Buddhism—are seen as instruments of evil: the temptress, seductress.) To perceive an object is to name it; to name an object is to objectify it, thus ever increasing our distance from the One. The poet uses language to transcend language, probably a losing proposition. What we cannot speak about, Wittgenstein tells us, we must pass over in silence. McClure: "Look at stanza 51. It begins in English and turns into beast language—star becomes stahr. Body becomes boody. Nose becomes noze. Everybody knows how to pronounce NOH or VOOR-NAH or GAHROOOOO ME."

Or, M. Merleau-Ponty. (Butterick has *Phenomenology of Perception,* trans. Colin Smith, in Olson's library, "Olson's Reading:

A Preliminary Report"): "I regard my body, which is my point of view upon the world, as one of the objects of that world. . . . Yet the absolute positing of a single object is the death of consciousness. . . . To be a consciousness or rather *to be an experience* is to hold inner communication with the world, the body and other people, to be with them instead of beside them." One of the central projects of phenomenological positivism, with its insistence on the ontological and epistemological primacy of perceptual experience, is the (re)instatement of the body as aperture. Poetry is a *muscular* principle, and it is only in the body (which includes, McClure reminds us, the mind: "intellect is a function of the body") that we are in the world. Again, Merleau-Ponty: "Our century has wiped out the dividing line between 'body' and 'mind'. . . . For many thinkers at the close of the nineteenth century, the body was a bit of matter, a network of mechanisms. The twentieth century has restored and deepened the notion of flesh, that is, of animate body" ("Man and Adversity"). We find this in Lao Tzu ("One who recognizes all people as members of one's own body / is sound to guard them"), Whitman/Thoreau/Emerson, and the New Physics. Duncan: "Merleau-Ponty sounded to me like some sections of my journals. . . . I find him almost impossible to read. He seems too redundant and robbing of my own thoughts" (Faas).

Aldous Huxley: "In Blake's words, we must 'cleanse the doors of perception'; for when the doors of perception are cleansed, everything appears to man as it is—infinite" ("Culture and the Individual"). Our current (USA, 1988) attitude towards drugs belies Merleau-Ponty's conclusion that in any actual sense— politically, socially, culturally—Cartesian dualism has been erased. The political hypocrisy/conspiracy of "just say no" is traced early in Alfred W. McCoy's *The Politics of Heroin in*

Southeast Asia (1972), which the CIA tried to suppress, and Allen Ginsberg's "Addiction Politics" (*Allen Verbatim,* 1974). Yet we know from R. Gordon Wasson that perhaps the (accidental) ingestion of a hallucinogenic plant, probably a Fly-agaric, led to our first recognition of deity. Certainly, under the influence of psilocybin, any notion of mind/body split is profoundly eased. Lawrence Lipton: Even ganja awakens us to recognition that "the magic circle is, in fact, a symbol of and a preparation for the metaphysical orgasm. While marijuana does not give the user the sense of timelessness to the same degree that peyote does, or LSD or other drugs, it does so sufficiently to impart a sense of *presence*" (*The Holy Barbarians*).

Psilocybin offers recognition of integration, McClure writes in "The Mushroom": "All of our notions of the human body's shape are wrong. We think it is a head joined on a torso and sprouting arms and legs and genitals or breasts, but we're wrong. It is more unified than that. It's one total unity of protoplasm." Or, more complexly to Meltzer, "All I am saying is we can grant recognition of that river within us which, in mixed vocabulary, could be the Hindu 'We are all one,' but it would seem that that doesn't lend any solution. I am many is where it is at. I am a heart, I am three trillion cells, I am a lung, I am many neuronal centers."

Timothy Leary: "1960. Allen Ginsberg phoned from New York, eager to begin our campaign for the politics of ecstasy. He had lined up mushroom sessions for Jack Kerouac, Robert Lowell, and Barney Rossett, famed avant-garde publisher. . . . Kerouac had propelled me into my first negative trip. . . . Throughout the night Kerouac had remained unmoveably the Catholic carouser, an old-style Bohemian without a hippie bone in his body. Jack Kerouac opened the neural doors to the future, looked ahead, and didn't see his place in it. Not for him the utopian pluralist optimisism of the sixties. . . . Lowell, always the gentleman, took me aside and wrung my hand in gratitude. 'Now I know what Blake and St. John of the Cross were talking about,' he said. 'This experience is what I was seeking when I became a Catholic'" (*Flashbacks*).

(Catholicism: Transubstantiation, the body into the body. Everson as Brother Antoninus; Rexroth's deathbed conversion; Duncan on Olson: "So Charles wanted to keep the Catholic origins somewhat in the same way that I kept my Hermeticism" [Faas]. All of McClure [a non-Catholic] 's network).

Snyder interview, 1974: "I've been really getting into botany. McClure got me started on learning plants more. It's so exciting to get through that initial kind of brush-tangle of taxonomy and get into seeing something."

1954, McClure meets Duncan, enrolling in his SF Poetry Center workshop. Two years earlier Duncan had taken mescalin ("the only time I took a hallucinogenic drug") in an experiment at Stanford (CIA sponsored?). His experience was typical, but unlike with McClure, Ginsberg, and Leary the revelation distressed him: "My sense of the external was so accute that I raised the question, as I still often do, whether there is any possible being in me which can be called my ego. . . . Later, in 1963, at the University of British Columbia, I gave a lecture which was about my refusal to have any mystical experiences because I wanted to be made out of thousands of threads that I myself have tied" (Faas).

Again, in 1958, Francis Crick purchased a copy of "Peyote Poem" broadside at Ferlinghetti's City Lights Bookstore in SF, written out of McClure's first experience with the drug, five buttons given him by the artist Wallace Berman, his "peyote father" ("The Beat Surface").

The dark brown space behind the door is precious
intimate, silent and still. The birthplace
of Brahms. I know
all that I need to know. There is no hurry.

In 1963 McClure writes of psilocybin, peyote, heroin, and cocaine; in 1982 he opens *Scratching the Beat Surface* with his "Peyote Poem" and narrative surrounding it. (In 1969, interviewed in Algiers, Eldridge Cleaver: "I will reenter [the United States], and I plan to shed my blood and to put my life on the line and to seek to take the lives of the pigs of the power structure in Babylon," *Conversations;* by the 1980s he had become a born-again Christian, working for a Christian broadcasting network.) "Revolt is a biological principle."

Mushroom: "It opens you up so that you feel internally deep inside, and all around you, the utterly human and humane. . . . People are no longer like our conception of them. They are like godly beasts."

Peyote: "Sharp divisions between inert and organic disappear. A spectrum and flow of intensities of spirit and life-meanings is visible. The life in 'inert' things is seen and the 'death' in organic things is visible."

Heroin: (The mention of the word evokes hysteria, yet physicians tell us that the substance has no effect on vital organs, unlike alcohol). "A new kind of self takes over—there is not so much *I*. I is an interference with near-passivity. . . . A loosening of ways of thinking and the visible beauties that things have when we are relaxed."

Cocaine: "An *ace of sunlight.*"

McClure's NET film: "I first took peyote because I heard it was great. . . . It was a divine experience. With another friend I went on a trip of investigating, taking all of it I could possibly get my hands on. What happened was that I took so many, so many times, that I began to have what I call 'the dark side of the soul,' and which Allen Ginsberg calls anxiety. The last time I took peyote it took six weeks to come down. In fact, I didn't know if I was ever going to come down. I walked up and down the street looking at the cracks in the sidewalk. . . . I vowed not to take any more hallucinogens. But then I did take one more, and I think I'm ready to take more now" (1966).

Reich's orgone experiments and McClure's experiments with drugs converge at the same vortex: poetry as muscular principle.

Allen Ginsberg on the poet's responsibility re: drug education: "And as the regular respectable professors refused to deal with that area—well, doctors and psychiatrists gave it over into the hands of the police, or the police grabbed it out of their hands. So it was left to some extent to the poets to formulate some sort of public knowledge, to transmit granny wisdom about those things" (1974, *The Beat Journey*).

McClure: "A crack of light must be made. There should be no lies. . . . There should be no mystiques of language, drugs, or sex, or . . . !" ("Heroin: A Cherub's Tale").

The New Book / Book of Torture—collection of poems written "in a psychedelic state": "I am a black beast and clear man in one. With no / split or division . . . / Free of politics. Liberty and pride to guide you. You pass / from ancestral myths to myth of self. And make / the giant bright stroke like that madman Van Gogh."

(<L *poema* < Gk *poema*, var. of *poiema* poem, something made = *poi [ein]* [to] make + −*ema* −EME.)

"Each Poem should be an experiment—in the sense that there are experiments in alchemy and biochemistry. I have my transient meatflesh to play on as if it is a harp. . . . A poem is an amino acid in the ripples of an endless sea" (*September Blackberries,* 1974).

The NET film, alone in a dark room, mid-summer afternoon. McClure is very young, very handsome, wearing the paisley shirt you saw everywhere that year in the Haight, at the Fillmore. "I wanted to make poetry that didn't have images in the sense the images describe something in the real world. But the sound of the poetry itself creates an image in the mind, the body, the muscles of the body. Created a melody that was also an image, that imprinted itself in the body."

He stands with the great lions at San Francisco's Fleishaker Zoo, those indoor cages I remember from childhood trips across the bay, lions surely long dead three decades later. He reads to them in beast language. "When a man does not admit that he is an animal. Ghrooooh!" They stir, and are roused.

Years after, he watches a snow leopardess. "She puts her face within an inch of the wire and SPEAKS to me. . . . I am surrounded by the physicality of her speech. It is a real thing in the air. It absorbs me and I can feel and see nothing else. Her face and features disappear, becoming one entity with her speech. The speech is the purest, most perfect music I have ever heard, and I know that I am touched by the divine, on my cheeks, and on my brow, and on the typanums of my ears, and the vibrations on my chest, and on the inner organs of perception. It is music-speech. . . . We see, hear, feel through the veil. WE are translated" ("A Mammal Gallery," 1982).

Poetics

YES! THERE IS BUT ONE
POLITICS AND THAT
IS BIOLOGY.
BIOLOGY
IS
POLITICS.
We dive into
the black, black rainbow

of the end
unless we spend
our life and build love
in creation of
what is organic.
The old views
(worn and blasted)
are a structure
of death.
Our breath
IS
TO
SERVE
THE ULTIMATE
beauty
of ourselves.

6 Outsiders as Insiders: The Idea of the West in the Work of Thom Gunn and Nathaniel Tarn

In his autobiographical essay, "Child as Father to Man in the American Uni-verse," Nathaniel Tarn opens with an intriguing anecdote:

> Last year I received a letter from a member of the English department at a university in Philadelphia. She informed me that she had been asked to write an article on my work for a prominent dictionary of literary biography. She had been working all summer and had been most impressed. Could we meet for detailed discussions? I called for a pleasant talk. After a while, she revealed that I was to be included in the volume on postwar British poets. I said that I had now been here twelve years, was a citizen, and had been a champion of American poetry, even in England, for ten years before that. She was very sorry. She had been preparing a conference paper as well. Her editor called later: would I not reconsider this "foolish casting away of a chance at an academic reputation?" I talked about the virtues of consistency. He put down the phone with a marked, sorrowful finality. A terminal case.[1]

"Yet, over the years," he concludes, "I had begun to wonder whether, once past the Statue of Liberty, the tired, poor, huddled and yearning poet stood a chance in hell of ever really being accepted in America." And more important, at least from the reader's point of view, accepted or not, just what effect would such a migration have on a poet (writing in Doris Sommer's phrase, as "outsider as insider"[2]) and his work?

The early part of this century saw American writers fleeing the provincialism of the United States for the cosmopolitan centers of London, Paris, and Rome. Henry James, Ezra Pound, Gertrude Stein, Ernest Hemingway, F. Scott Fitzgerald, T. S. Eliot, and so many others looked to England and the Continent for a kind of emotional and creative regeneration. At mid-century, at least among the English, the migration reversed itself a bit, with such figures as Christopher Isherwood and Aldous Huxley locating permanently in southern California, and W. H. Auden becoming a United States citizen. Of the three most accomplished contemporary poets to emigrate from England to the United States—Denise Levertov, Thom Gunn, and Nathaniel Tarn—two, Gunn and Tarn, have significantly addressed the ethos of the West in their work; here I would like to discuss the nature of that address.

Though born a year later than Tarn, Gunn emigrated to the United States first, in 1954, to study with Yvor Winters at Stanford. Spending a year in Texas shortly after, he settled in San Francisco in 1960, where he still lives, a member of the English Department faculty at the University of California at Berkeley. Tarn, more peripatetic, first traveled to the United States in 1951, as a Smith-Mundt-Fulbright scholar in anthropology at the University of Chicago. Following a return to London, and extensive travels in Guatemala and Burma, he immigrated permanently to the United States in 1970, living for the next decade in Pennsylvania as a professor of comparative literature at Rutgers. Since 1984, Tarn has resided in northern New Mexico.

Before taking up residency in California, Gunn published a book in England, *Fighting Terms* (1954; revised edition 1958); before making his move to Pennsylvania, Tarn published four collections of poetry: *Old Savage/Young City* (1964), *Where Babylon Ends* (1968), *The Beautiful Contradictions* (1969), and *October* (1970). These early volumes were widely reviewed in England. Anthony Thwaite regarded Gunn's work as "poems of self-discovery and passionate but disciplined inquiry," while John Fuller saw the poems as examples of a new "vigor and clarity." Of Tarn's *Old Savage,* Elizabeth Jennings wrote that the poems were "taut and virile . . . a very fine, vigorous first book," while Martin Seymour-Smith found the work "insidiously exciting," and Danny Abse argued that "a truly interesting poet has arrived upon the scene." Gunn's work was quickly picked up by the prestigious firm of Faber and Faber, while later Tarn's could be found in *Encounter, Stand, Agenda,* and the *TLS.* In short, from the start both Gunn and Tarn were regarded as important new voices whose poetic careers in England were assured. Why then leave England for the United States?

For Gunn, the move seems to have been prompted as much by personal as aesthetic reasons. As he explains in his short essay, "My Life Up To Now," while a student at Cambridge he had met

> Mike Kitay, an American, who became the leading
> influence on my life, and thus on my poetry. It is
> not easy to speak of a relationship so long-lasting, so
> deep, and so complex, nor of the changes it has gone
> through, let alone of the effect it had on my writing. . . . I found that the only way to get to the

United States, where I intended to eventually join
Mike (who had to go into the air force) was to get a
fellowship at some university.[3]

Donald Hall suggested that he apply for a creative-writing
fellowship at Stanford, which he received; thus at the age of
twenty-five, he left London for Palo Alto, California, to study
under Yvor Winters, "with whose very name I was unfamil-
iar."

"Well, I am gay," Gunn told a group of graduate students
at the University of New Mexico in 1983. "I suppose that the
early nonappearance of overtly gay subject matter in my poetry
had to do with the taboos, even the laws of the time. It was very
difficult being gay in the 1950s and 1960s."[4] In the same interview Gunn explained that he loves "northern California, and
almost as soon as I got there I knew it would be my home. I
can't think of any good literary reasons." In fact, given the
development of his poetry over the past two decades, we will
soon see that actually there have been good "literary reasons"
for his remaining in California. However, obviously at least at
first probably the primary reason for remaining in the Bay Area
was Gunn's sense that it was simply easier being gay there than
in London.

> I went several times into San Francisco. It was still
> something of an open city, with whore-houses flour-
> ishing for anybody to see. A straight couple took
> me to my first gay bar, the Black Cat. It excited me
> so much that the next night I returned there on my
> own. And I remember walking along Columbus
> Avenue on another day, thinking that the ultimate
> happiness would be for Mike and me to settle in this
> city.[5]

"If England is my parent," he wrote, "San Francisco is my
lover."

Further, the poet Robert Duncan, who lived at the time in the East Bay and became a close friend, offered Gunn a kind of model. "Homosexuality was held in particular horror even by liberals who would not have dreamed of attacking other minorities," Gunn wrote in his essay "Homosexuality in Robert Duncan's Poetry."[6] "In the mid-fifties, when I asked my teacher and friend Yvor Winters why he did not like Whitman's poem about the twenty-eight young men bathing (*Song of My-self*, 11), he replied that the homosexual feeling of the poem was such that he could not get beyond it." While most other gay writers declined to deal directly with the question of sexual orientation in their work (Auden and Gunn both used, for example, "an unspecified 'you,'" giving an occasional ambiguous hint about what was really going on to those in the know only"), as early as 1944 Duncan had publicly and aggressively announced his homosexuality in "The Homosexual in Society," an essay in *Politics,* a journal edited by Dwight Macdonald. This pronouncement was not without cost; John Crowe Ransom, who had accepted Duncan's "African Elegy" for publication in the *Kenyon Review,* angrily withdrew the acceptance, accusing Duncan of "homosexual advertisement." But from Gunn's point of view, Duncan had achieved a kind of archetypal American freedom, had staked out new and unexplored territory. "He could speak about his sexuality openly but with barely any twentieth-century tradition of such openness behind him. . . . It is due more to Duncan," Gunn concluded, "than to any other single poet that Modern American poetry, in all its exclusiveness, can deal with overtly homosexual material so much as a matter of course—not as something perverse or eccentric or morbid, but as evidence of the many available ways in which people live their lives, of the many available ways in which people love or fail to love."[7]

This freedom represented by the ethos of San Francisco

and Duncan worked to open up for Gunn both his subject matter and his technique. While at Cambridge, Gunn had read Chaucer, Shakespeare, and Donne, as well as modern writers such as Auden, Sartre, and Camus. And yet, when he arrived at Stanford he was almost oblivious to the work of modern American poets.

> I couldn't get hold of the obvious American poets
> let alone the less obvious ones. If I had wanted to
> read William Carlos Williams in 1954, I'd have had
> to go to some extremely well-stocked library with
> American editions. There were no English editions
> of Williams. No English editions of Hart Crane.
> The first *selected* poems by Wallace Stevens came out
> in England in 1954. The English were very late in
> publishing the American poets.[8]

The poems in his first commercially published book, *Fighting Terms,* were written from 1951 to 1953, under the influence of Cambridge. Gunn has recognized in these poems a debt to the major English writers, especially the Elizabethans, "but they were writers I could see as bearing upon the present, upon my own activities. Donne and Shakespeare spoke a living language to me, and it was one I tried to turn to my own uses." Further, there is a certain distance, a certain objectivity here, a sense of dramatic form. "At Cambridge as undergraduates people were doing really astonishing performances of Shakespeare, and I'm sure it was an important influence on me. There I was in the 1950s thinking about heroic action, which is what I tried to get into *Fighting Terms.*"[9] And, of course, all the poems are written according to strict metrical (usually iambic pentameter) and rhyming patterns, as announced in the opening stanza of the first poem in the volume, "The Wound":

The huge wound in my head began to heal
About the beginning of the seventh week.
Its valleys darkened, its villages became still:
For joy I did not move and dared not speak;
Not doctors would cure it, but time, its patient skill.

Thirty-five years later, most of these poems seem apprentice pieces, and are generally conventional and predictable, owing obviously much to Auden. There are numerous literary references and allusions: Troy, Lazarus, Leda, Shelley, Shakespeare. Further, Gunn had developed a "theory" akin to the notion of persona: "The theory of pose was this: everyone plays a part, whether he knows it or not, so he might as well deliberately design a part, or a series of parts, for himself . . . trying to play a part provided rich material for poetry."[10] A number of these poems are dramatically conceived, the speaker first a warrior, then a lover, then a hawk; and as the title implies, often the stance of the speaker is aggressive, a modern Odysseus.

Recently Gregory Woods has argued that the martial aspect of many of Gunn's early poems is sexual.[11] In the New Mexico interview, Gunn admits that the martial figure, the soldier, "came to stand for all role players. Wearing a uniform is much like playing a role." There are a number of love poems in this collection—"Lofty in the Palais de Danse," "La Prisonnière," "Carnal Knowledge," "Without a Counterpart"—but there is no indication to the general reader that these poems are other than conventional heterosexual address. In fact, the opening of a poem like "Carnal Knowledge" (which led off the first edition of the book but was moved further in with the revised edition), while explicitly acknowledging the "pose," could hardly be read otherwise:

Even in bed I pose: desire may grow
More circumstantial and less circumspect

Each night, but an acute girl would suspect
My thoughts might not be, but like my body, bare.
I wonder if you know, or, knowing, care?
You know I know you know I know you know.

And yet, Gunn tells his lover (and his reader), "I am not what I seem." And even an erotic poem written more than a decade later, "Touch," offers no overt clue to the speaker's homosexuality: "You are already / asleep. I lower / myself in next to / you, my skin slightly / numb with the restraint / of habits, the patina of / self, the black frost / of outsideness. . . . "

By the late seventies, however, Gunn's work opened up to a far more direct, self-revelatory address. A poem like "Bally Power Play" is overtly homoerotic in its description of the "pinball wizard" who caught in "the abstract drama of the ball," is "the cool source of all that hurry / and desperate activity, in control, legs apart, braced arms apart."

Between games
he recognizes me, we chat,
he tells me about broken promises
with comic-rueful smile
at his need for reassurance,
which is as great as anybody's.
He once told me he never starts
to look for the night's partner
until half an hour before closing time.
The rest is foreplay.

In "New York" (included, like "Bally Power Play," in *The Passages of Joy*), the narrator sees "my dear host in the bed and / his Newfoundland on it, together / stretching, half-woken, as / I close the door. / I calm down, / undress, and slip / in between them and think / of household gods," while in "Sweet Things," of a "scrubbed cowboy, Tom Sawyer," he exclaims, "How handsome he is in / his lust and energy, in his / fine display of impulse . . . / My boy / I could eat you whole."

Thus, here we see not only a more explicit homoeroticism, but also a major shift in Gunn's sense of narrative stance. Replacing the "dramatic poses" of the early English poems—so typical of the conservative formalist practice of poets like Auden and the early Lowell—in this later work Gunn and the narrative "I" are obviously one in the same. *Fighting Terms's* warrior and hawk (the Eliotic personae behind which the poet was carefully positioned) here are reduced to the poet himself— his direct experiences and his meditations on those experiences. "I think the greater openness had something to do with gay liberation," Gunn reasons, "maybe with the influence of San Francisco itself." Once he had settled in the West, he "began to get more interested in personal experience, though you have to remember that when you are young you just don't have so much personal experience to think about. At that time you madly want to fall in love so that you'll have some love poetry to write."[12] And again, it seems to have been not only time but location providing for Gunn a set of particularly striking experiences which offered a poetics that moved progressively more into the personal.

From the start Gunn seems to have been drawn to figures of physical prowess ("I think of all the toughs through history / And thank heaven they lived, continually. / I praise the overdogs from Alexander / To those who would not play with Stephen Spender"), though as his work develops these figures are drawn more and more archetypally American, and are usually members of one counterculture or another. Probably his most well-known poem, "On the Move," leads off his second collection, *The Sense of Movement,* a book composed of thirty-two poems written primarily after his arrival at Stanford.

On the motorcycles, up the road, they come:
Small, black, as flies hanging in the heat, the Boys,
Until the distance throws them forth, their hum
Bulges to thunder held by calf and thigh.
In goggles, donned impersonality
In gleaming jackets trophied with the dust,
They strap in doubt—by hiding it, robust—
And almost hear a meaning in their noise.

In their leather, the Boys live not a life born of convention and
the burden of history, but rather are "self-defined, astride the
created will." As Alan Bold points out in his study of Gunn and
Ted Hughes, in both this poem and many others in the volume,
"there is an obsessional interest in the will," as it becomes "the
machine that drives the body into action" in quest of an "identity."[13] And certainly again in "The Unsettled Motorcyclist's
Vision of His Death," the countercultural hero, the outlaw,
rebels against integration as his "human will cannot submit / To
nature, though brought out of it."

As in the Unsettled Motorcyclist's vision, the fine line
between the human and animal domains holds particular interest for Gunn. Elvis Presley appears, like an incipient werewolf,
with "crawling sideburns," turning "revolt into a style," while
the "wolf boy" strains against the moon's loosing of "desires
hoarded against his will / . . . he has bleeding paws." Not only
is such a figuring an obvious reference to the dual life the
homosexual must by convention lead, but as Bold notes in this
last poem in particular the primary image is that of "civilized
English life acting like a vicious trap to squeeze all impulse and
instinct out of the individual."[14] The only hope of escape is
through the outlaw will, to somehow define oneself outside the
expectations of convention.

Gunn's fullest expression of this theme occurs in his 1971
volume *Moly,* the first of his books to show a sustained Ameri-

can influence. The physical setting for most of these poems
(when they can be placed) is northern California: "The Bay, the
Gate, the Bridge" of "The Sand Man"; the "Pacific's touch" of
"Three"; the Haight-Ashbury of "Street Song"; Marin's "landscape of acid" of "The Fair in the Woods"; "Listening to Jefferson Airplane" in Golden Gate Park; Kirby Cove's "laurel and
eucalyptus, dry sharp smells" of "Grasses"; Folsom Street's
"Hamm's Brewery, a huge blond glass / Filling as its compe-
nent lights are lit" of "At the Centre";

> They lean against the cooling car, backs pressed
> Upon the dusts of a brown continent,
> And watch the sun, now Westward of their West,
> Fall to the ocean. Where it led they went.

of "the Discovery of the Pacific."

More important, the psychological setting offers a kind of
expansive consciousness which we've come to identify with the
West Coast, and in particular a serious examination of the
transformative powers of hallucinogenic drugs as a stay against
the "English trap." As he recounts in his autobiographical essay,
he had spent about a year in London, finding that with the
popularity of the Beatles "barriers seemed to be coming down
all over," though the counterculture in San Francisco "was
prepared to go much further."

> It was the time, after all, not only of the Beatles but
> of LSD as well. Raying out from the private there
> was a public excitement at the new territories that
> were being opened up in the mind. Golden Gate
> Park, the scene of so many mass trips and rock con-
> certs, seemed like "The first field of a glistening
> continent / Each found by trusting Eden in the hu-
> man." We tripped also at home, on rooftops, at
> beaches and ranches, some went to opera loaded on

acid, others tried it as passengers on gliders, every experience was illuminated by the drug. . . . These were the fullest years of my life, crowded with discovery both inner and outer, as we moved between ecstasy and understanding. It is no longer fashionable to praise LSD, but I have no doubt at all that it has been of the utmost importance to me, both as a man and a poet.[15]

Though he felt that "the acid experience was essentially non-verbal," he learned things about himself that he had "somehow blocked from my own view." Most of the poems in *Moly*, "written between 1965 and 1970, have in some way however indirect to do with it." And the finest poems in the collection— "Rites of Passage," "Moly," "Tom Dobbin," and "At the Centre"—are directly related to Gunn's LSD experiences.

Again, in "Moly," the poet focuses on the line between human and animal:

> I root and root, you think that it is greed,
> It is, but I seek out a plant I need.

> Direct me gods, whose changes are holy,
> To where it flickers deep in grass, the moly:

> Cool flesh of magic in each leaf and shoot,
> From milky flower to the black forked root.

> From this fat dungeon I could rise to skin
> And human title, putting pig within.

> I push my big grey wet snout through the green,
> Dreaming the flower I have never seen.

Gunn tells us that he "wanted the poem to be grotesque."[16] Like Kafka's Gregor Samsa, he has awakened from sleep to find himself transformed; "but what kind of animal is it? Is this leathery hide? Or feathery? Or scales? What have I become? I know I'm not a man any longer." He has exchanged conventional perception for a deeper, yet potentially more threatening, vision, the "nightmare of beasthood, snorting."

In a review of *The Oxford Book of Twentieth Century Verse,* Auden argued that "Nature to the English is a friendly mother-earth whom we can trust. To the Americans, on the other hand, nature has been virgin and hostile, a *dura virum nutrix* to be subdued by force."[17] While as in "The Fair in the Woods" Gunn perceives nature as rather pastoral and passive (and even there we get a hint of danger in the poem's closing image, "In the autumnal dusk, for it is late. / The horns call. There is little left to shine"), generally LSD draws him to that archetypal American dichotomy of being at once drawn toward and terrified by the natural world. Of one LSD experience in particular (the genesis of "At the Centre"), Gunn says, it was "one of those extraordinary trips where you really don't set out to meet God, maybe don't believe in him, but there he was anyway."[18] The setting here is the Hamm's Beer Brewery on Folsom Street in San Francisco, a factory which for years was famous for the large sign in the shape of a beer glass which rested on the roof and appeared to fill and empty through a series of lights. For Gunn, the factory becomes somehow emblematic of this split consciousness—"What place is this / Cracked wood steps led me here":

> Terror and beauty in a single board.
> The rough grain in relief—a tracery
> Fronded and ferned, of woods inside the wood.
> Splinter and scar—I saw them too, they poured.
> White paint-chip and the overhanging sky:
> The flow-lines faintly traced or understood.

As in "Rites of Passage," the vision is at once lucent ("My blood, it is like light. / Behind an almond bough") and terrible ("your groin's trembling warns. / I stamp upon the earth / A message to my mother. / And then I lower my horns").

One would expect the structure of such drug-induced visionary poems to be rather open, as, for example, in Allen Ginsberg's "Mescaline" and "Lysergic Acid." Yet in fact, Gunn explains, for him

> Metre seemed to be the proper form for the LSD-related poems, though at first I didn't understand why. Later I rationalized about it thus. The acid trip is unstructured, it opens you up to countless possibilities, you hanker after the infinite. The only way I could give myself any control over the presentation of these experiences, and so could be true to them, was by trying to render the infinite through the finite, the unstructured through the structured. Otherwise there was the danger of the experience's becoming so distended that it would simply unravel like a fog before wind in the unpremediated movement of free verse.[19]

Thus "Rites of Passage," *Moly*'s lead poem, is a series of four rhymed iambic sestets, "Moly" fourteen iambic pentameter rhymed couplets, and so on. And certainly Gunn is perceptive in his choice here, as we feel the material, the pulse of the human will warring against the animal, straining against the civilizing boundaries of fixed form.

Gunn's sense of form remains a kind of enigma. The hallmark of postmodern American poetry, and most especially the poetry of the principal West Coast writers like Kenneth Rexroth, Robert Duncan, and William Everson, has been not only the opening up of subject matter and new areas of consciousness, but also, even perhaps centrally, the opening up of form. Yet such an opening up of form has seemingly affected Gunn's work only subtly and occasionally. Like other English Movement poets (Philip Larkin, Donald Davie, D. J. Enright) early on Gunn conceived of poetry in neoclassical terms—the artist was to be first a craftsman, adept at inherited form. As I mentioned earlier, the poems collected in *Fighting Terms* are all formally constructed, using primarily iambic pentameter and offering various rhyme patterns.

Gunn sees this question as a distinguishing factor between English and American poets.

> The English poets are still in love with meter and rhyme, and you don't get many of them writing good free verse. On the other hand, you don't get many American poets writing good meter and rhyme. There is a loss on both sides. British poetry and American poetry do seem to have grown much farther apart during the last ten or fifteen years. For a brief period, in the 1950's, they had been coming closer together and enriching each other, but they don't seem to be learning from each other at the moment, or even have much of anything in common.[20]

D. H. Lawrence, another emigrè, offers a model in his *Collected Poems,* a volume which contains "about half metrical and half free-verse poems." The point of the book's preface, Gunn argues, "is that free-verse is poetry of the present, while metrical verse is poetry of the past and future." Certainly the form of most of Gunn's work is conventional; it is not until his 1966 volume, *Positives* (with photographs by his brother Ander), that he makes any kind of serious venture into free verse. While the poems in the next book, *Touch,* are also primarily unrhymed, still Gunn feels, as he explained above, by *Moly* the need to return to the tensions of rhyme. In the most recent books, *Jack Straw's Castle* and *The Passages of Joy,* he offers Lawrence's fusion of sensibilities to an extent—giving us a mix of rhymed and unrhymed work—though even there many of the unrhymed poems are syllabically regular.

Certainly, Gunn's replacing of his early dramatic "posing" with a focus on the personal, his poetry's dawning acceptance of overt homoeroticism, his immersion in the San Francisco counterculture (and, in particular, the prominance of LSD as an integral part of that culture), and both San Francisco and the coast landscape as evocative settings all have made available for Gunn numerous possibilities for a poetry perhaps more resonant than any of his contemporaries who remained in England. Yet most of the poet's finest work—"On the Move," "The Unsettled Motorcyclist's Vision of His Death," "Misanthropos," "Rites of Passage," "Moly"—relies on a conventional English formalism for its power. Given Gunn's own distinction between English and American poets, his unwillingness to embrace fully the open verse aesthetic of writers like Rexroth and Duncan makes any final assessment of his "Americanness" extremely problematic, and perhaps offers us a telling clue as to which tradition, his many years in northern California notwithstanding, he regards as his own. The lover provides matter, approach, occasion; but the parent, Gunn's primary prosody would imply, imprints a kind of grounding which is ineluctable.

If Gunn has accepted the western ethos as a fertile geography for the nurturing of a poetry which remains at its heart English, long before he actually left England Nathaniel Tarn began to adopt the American ethos—both in his subjects and in his prosody—as a conscious alternative to what he perceived as a stagnant literary scene. As he recounts in his "Uni-verse" essay, he felt "English poetry had been dead since Hopkins at best, or since Blake at worst," and that whatever power British (over against English) poetry had in this century was resident in Celtic poets like Yeats, MacDiarmid, and Thomas.[21] Tarn felt that, because of his status as "an international wandering mestizo, additionally Jewish," the English language "could therefore live for me in a new country, a chosen country," the United States.

Tarn's first "career" was in anthropology rather than poetry, writing and teaching under the heteronym E. Michael Mendelson. Born in Paris, he was educated at Cambridge, the Ecole des Hautes Etudes, and the London School of Economics; he received a Ph.D. in anthropology from the University of Chicago with a dissertation on Guatemalan "religion and world-view," and until 1967 he worked as a lecturer in Southeast Asian anthropology at the School of Oriental and African Studies, University of London. Though he had written poetry sporadically since his childhood, much of it in French, it wasn't until doing anthropological fieldwork in Burma in 1959 that he began to write seriously with an eye toward publication. "While in Burma," he recalls,

> I had met a young lecturer, a Canadian poet who had lived in London a few years. He had been involved with some English poets who had formed a meeting-ground called "The Group." This was basically a bunch of people surrounding Edward Lucie-Smith, meeting at his home every Friday night to discuss the poems of one particular person. It took this poet friend of mine about a year and a half or so to introduce me into that gathering. . . . One of the poets in "The Group" was George MacBeth, who was also an influential program director at the BBC. The BBC came up with the proposal that one of "The Group" nights should be broadcast as a program, and I was chosen by Lucie-Smith as the poet. . . . I sent the poems to a lot of people, including T. S. Eliot, though I knew his anti-semitic attitude might stand in the way of a reading. But I just

> sent them all over London. Things got rolling very
> fast, and poems started appearing here and there,
> mainly in places run by friends of "The Group."[22]

In 1963 Tarn won the Guinness Prize for Poetry, and soon after his first book, *Old Savage/Young City,* was published by Jonathan Cape. Four years later he resigned his lectureship at London University to join Cape Goliard as founding general editor of Cape Editions. In 1970, following publication of three more full-length collections of poetry, he emigrated permanently to the United States.

Tarn admits that his third book, *The Beautiful Contradictions,* published the year before he left England, "is probably the book I'd choose to begin my opus with. . . . The whole question of scope was very important to my trying to get out of the attitude of 'Little Englandism' in 'The Movement' and, later, 'The Group.' " Though Tarn's first two books are far less conventional than *Fighting Terms,* Tarn himself regards them as rather false starts: "Despite the Americawards title poem of the first book, *Old Savage/Young City,* and its successor, *Where Babylon Ends,* they must probably be accounted, stylistically and structurally, as English books. The people I remember feeling close to at this time were poets such as Christopher Middleton, David Wevill, some of Peter Redgrove and Jon Silkin, as well as younger writers, more American-influenced, like Tom Raworth and Lee Harwood, and poet-artists like John Digby, my close friend."[23]

Stylistically, the poems of *Savage* are certainly far more open than Gunn's early poems; Tarn works through no traditional forms, there is no rhyme, there is no regular meter. (We must remember that though the book appeared a full decade after Gunn's, the formalist aesthetic was still little challenged in England.) A few of the poems, like "Blackfly Melting," use short lines, while most, like "Abulafia at the Gates of Rome, A.D. 1280," are composed of rather unusually long lines:

> From Saragossa to Safed the world groans with
>   my friends
> who drain themselves daily with the wine of the
>   Holy Name,
> yet for years I have not met with them nor wept
>   on their arms.
> Let each one wake with me now under these
>   stubborn gates.

Unlike in the poems of *Fighting Terms,* capitals are reserved for the start of each syntactic unit rather than the start of each line. Yet, this work is hardly innovative; the poems have the feeling of constraint, and certainly the diction is often self-conscious and literary ("grief is so much a now," "three doves, O whiteness manifest, purl wings," "she thinks herself a ship, tempest-split"), the idiom obviously British ("queueing to get past a muddy patch that pram wheels / keep dry"). Like Gunn's first poems, here each seems a well-wrought lyric or narrative argument, and the subjects are fairly traditional; further, while a few exotic settings are invoked, most of the poems' landscapes are nonspecific.

Tarn's third English volume, *The Beautiful Contradictions,* was written a year before he left for the United States. Unlike the two previous collections of short poems, *Contradictions* is a long poem of fifteen sections, with endnotes. According to the poet, Hugh MacDiarmid was a central influence:

> At some stage during the composition of *Contradic-*
> *tions,* a reading by MacDiarmid was announced in
> London, and I suddenly realized that I hadn't read
> him. I started right away, went to the reading, and

undertook an epic venture to his home outside of
Edinburgh. My reading convinced me that Mac-
Diarmid was a giant on the British horizon. He be-
longed to the Celtic fringe, which I saw as more
alive than the English. He was this huge mountain
on which the little English sheep were grazing; they
couldn't even see the mountain, it was so big.
Neruda and Pound were there, of course, but it was
MacDiarmid who gave me this feeling that there
was nothing in the world that couldn't be discussed
in poetic terms.[24]

And perhaps most significantly, this encounter offered "above
all that impetus which changed my breath line and enabled me
to bring in my anthropological experience. My life got into
Beautiful Contradictions in a way that it hadn't in the previous
books because of MacDiarmid's example. Robert Duncan later
remarked on that in a letter."

It seems to me that there was perhaps as great an influence
on the subject and structure of the poem to be found in Gloucester, Massachusetts, as in Biggar, Lanarkshire, however, as by
this time, Tarn had also read the work of Charles Olson closely.
As general editor of Cape editions, the poet had acquired rights
to Olson's *Call Me Ishmael* and *Mayan Letters* (he considered
Duncan and Zukofsky the other two of his "three pillars"). In
terms of the poetry, he was drawn not so much to *Maximus* "as
the earlier poet of *The Distances,* which seemed to me, at the
time, linguistically the most invigorating book of the post-
Poundian era."[25] Certainly, Tarn's reference to the focus on
"breath line" is a conscious echo of Olson's dictum in "Projective Verse" (a reaction to mainstream English prosody and its
influence on American poetry) that "verse now, 1950, if it is to
go ahead, if it is to be of essential use, must, I take it, catch up
and put into itself certain laws and possibilities of the breath";

further, Olson offered a model for the fusion of poetic and anthropological interests in his work on Mayan glyphs.

Like "The Kingfishers" (probably the central poem of *The Distances*), *Contradictions* offers in its prosody innovative line lengths and breath spacings, as well as an attempt to see connections between cultures (including most especially the "primitive") and ages. As Tarn mentions in his endnotes, the poem is intended to move from "primitive innocence" through "every shade of complexity to the exhaustion of human capacities," ending with "a new simplicity," a kind of "non-attachment." Much of the poem's imagery is drawn from the Americas (particularly Guatemala), and Tarn's interest here is at least in part making that culture as living a worldview for us as Kung's China was for Pound. "An anthropologist is often torn between his desire to preserve what he studies and his knowledge that the clock can never be turned back," he continues in the notes. "For him, scientific records serve as a formal constraint, as well as a point of departure, for the imagination and faithful topography may be very near to the concept of justice." This "scientific record" works as a fascinating structural device, a kind of rhyming of data which sets the boundaries for the poem's movement, establishes its "field."

Certainly Tarn's richest and most complex poem is the long *Lyrics for the Bride of God,* written over his first five years in the United States and published in 1975. One of the most striking aspects of *Contradictions* is the privileging of the feminine, the "mother as the abiding reality" or, in *Bride,* "a female aspect of God." The poems you are about to hear," Tarn tells us in the verse preface to *Bride,* "belong to the time of wandering . . . / Something has happened. Someone has arrived. I am not alone. / The arrival may best be spoken of as a she. Perhaps. I may call her the Friend. / She is what I thought of as my own presence. The heart's is her weight." Like the narrator of *Con-*

traditions, Tarn's Bride ranges freely through cultures and time, and like the archetypal American new Adam is a chameleon of identity, race, and age.

The poem's method is primarily that of *Paterson* and *Maximus,* paratactic without closure, and one of its central movements is "America," a passage comprising eleven parts. It is in this section of the poem Tarn finds his permanent "home," as here the image of America holds center stage, both as setting and idea. The particular location (and where Tarn himself is at the time living) is New Hope, Pennsylvania, though the city's name itself seems a bit ironic as the poet looks out his back yard at tourists, "souls of no country, owning everything. The trash waits for them in the stores . . . coating their arteries like a slime." The new hope of the new land seems at first reduced to a cash nexus. Yet the next many sections of the poem offer in their lyricism a far more positive, far richer perspective as the "bird" of America flies from the East (an extension of the Old World) to points north, south, and west. As the poem progresses, the male poet finds himself a child in "the garden," as "the father is a child again at his daughter's feet . . . relearning his parts." Like New Hope, New York, as "the great bitch" who "talks about freedoms she has not attained," offers only the crassest materialism: "sports-busses / electronic shavers / telephoto record-players." Again it is western space (though "wasted prairie") which attracts him, as "the old-world systems" are "exhausted." Looking west, like Whitman the poet is "full this morning of democratic vistas,"

> it was like an indigo sky at night, star-studded,
> and the gates were opening out while they planted
>   the race
> leading into the Ideal Republic of Pacific America
> the very furthest far western West that anyone could
>   conceive

—a "West" which "came to be called Paradiso Terrestre after those who had gone before."

Appropriately, the "America" passage concludes with a visit to Charles Olson's Gloucester, and a kind of a baptism:

> We went down to the sea
> all the poets together
> and gave ourselves up to the waters
>   in various positions of loss:
> I realized that I had never died into water
>   and within five minutes
> after giving myself completely to the wave

he is renewed, "all the fear was gone." Like Gunn, here Tarn comes to an acceptance of the new land's dual nature, though with a difference. America's terror is human, bodied forth in the political institutions which "killed Allende for instance / has killed Neruda," the institutions which "repeat Spain." It is nature and the land itself, however, which offer regenerative possibilities, the "first shores," the "Adam-hut":

> Swallow on the air
> mackerel in the sky
> mackerel in the water
> swallows on the sea
>   stitching silver to silver
> in the heart's water:
>   I am so glad to be home!

From this point on Tarn's work becomes as much as anything a dialogue with America (not only the continental United States, but Mexico, Central America, and Alaska), as he attempts to come to terms with his new land. The poems in *The House of Leaves,* for example, are for the most part set in the Americas—Santiago, Wyoming, Vancouver Island, Baja California, Bolinas—and are dedicated primarily to U.S. writers—

Kenneth Rexroth, Gary Snyder, Jerome and Diane Rothenberg, David Meltzer, Robert Duncan, Guy Davenport. In "An-
niversary: In a *Lyric's* Margin," Tarn senses his move to be
permanent, an entry into a new maturity ("I have closed the
door behind me . . . / was it to be / America then / the new
life, / —fall from the nest"), while in "Still Love, With Re-
public," he tells "L.W." that

> You and I
> for different but equivalent reasons,
> are the last two on earth to believe in
>   manifest destiny:
> we would like our poem to tell
> tourists in New Hope and Santa Fe
> something else about our aging country than bargains.
> Now once upon America shall we hold hands
> as if we were two coasts with the whole land between!

Again the image of the tourist appears as if to stress that Tarn
himself, always in the past a sojourner rather than a mere
tourist, has now settled in. By the 1979 *Alashka,* a set of poems
coauthored with Janet Rodney written out of the pair's experiences in Alaska, the vision of the American West has become
central:

> As we drove West, wasting the miles behind us
> willingly, putting great space between ourselves and
> anything that bound us to a place: the stubborn re-
> fusal of sentences to form, of the land to take shape,
> of the future to obey our will, as it had obeyed it up
> till now, the great land desiring to remain open, and
> unexperienced, refusing definition from the start, to
> be worked thru and thru, mile by mile, without
> complexity . . .

again echoing Olson's sense of the primary American archetype ("I take SPACE to be the central fact to man born in America"), as well as reiterating the fresh and boundless possibilities for a new life and a new art offered by this land the poet has chosen for his own.

Tarn's recent resettling in the high desert of Tesuque, New Mexico, simply completes in actual fact the move to the Far West he had already made psychologically and aesthetically. His interest in indigenous cultures, for example, has continued unabated, as he continues to strike a balance between "the recording angel and the creative angel. . . . It's like being married to two women. There's a wonderful Alec Guiness film where he is a sea captain with a wife in each of two ports; in the middle of his course he switches the photographs. That's the kind of tension I feel."[26] Since at least *Contradictions,* Tarn has remained interested (along with poets like Gary Snyder and Jerome Rothenberg) in the whole question of "ethno-poetics," and in 1970 he was involved with Rothenberg and Denis Tedlock in the founding of *Alcheringa,* an influential journal which attempted to fuse poetic and anthropological consciousness. Like Rothenberg and Snyder, Tarn found the current language of anthropology "alienated," and one of his primary projects has become the search for a new, more open and resolving poetic language:

> I have always been fascinated by the interplay between restricted and elaborated codes, between common parlances and formal rhetorics. Form is usually allowed to grow out of content, though I am aware of moving towards more and more open form as I discover that there is less that cannot be discussed in poetry. In the early work, my anthropological experience prompted me to speak out of various personae associated with *Old Savage:* an old,

wise Amerindian or Melasian, aware of what our
culture has done to his, forgiving, sad at his own destruction principally because it mirrors the destruction of the whole natural earth. Dropping
anthropology as a profession has enabled me to
speak as an anthropologist and add the dialectic of
observer and observed to the previous one-
dimensional picture.[27]

His work in books like *Bride* has thus alternated between political concerns and "simple lyrical-erotic sequences," as "the aim
is to work towards more and more satisfactory resolutions of
the tension between simplicity and complexity." And of course
such an attempt has been at the center of the strongest tradition
in American verse in this century, from Pound, Williams, and
Olson to Rexroth and Snyder.

The titles of Tarn's two most recent books of poetry, *The
Desert Mothers* and *At the Western Gates,* indicate the extent to
which he has embraced his new western geography as poetic
idea. Here the western landscape—the New Mexican desert,
the Alaskan coast and backcountry, Palenque—is more than
merely accidental setting; rather, the West itself often becomes a
primary thematic concern as the poet adjusts to his new life
with his female lover. In "Peredur West," for instance, he returns to his sense of the West as both home and female, as
"Motherwards he moves, back to his homeland, / the lady
leading him has promised it: / he grants her trust implicitly."
Here movement through the land itself offers yet another regeneration: "Facing the mesas jagged like a saw, / with teeth fit
for a giant's grinding jaw, / he now moves further west. / Even
so, travel helps the weary poet / moving a song back to his
heart." And again and again, in poems like "North Rim,"
"Animal Bride," and especially "The White Widow," the West
holds out for him a new focus of vision. "Hold up our hands to

the light," he writes in his elegiac prose poem for Kenneth Rexroth,

> The small black personage dances on our palms with her elegant legs lifting above our lines of fate. She grows transparent and, while your voice changes on, becomes almost invisible. Then she is visible again, bone white in the relentless desert air that leaves no room for anything but clarity.

7 ⚙ Theory of the Flower: Michael Palmer, Ron Silliman, and Language Poetry

1. Palmer's Wittgenstein

> "The common behavior of mankind is the system of reference by means of which we interpret an unknown language."
>
> *Philosophical Investigations*

Michael Palmer, reviewing John Ashbery's *Shadow Train* (*Sulfur*, 4), is acutely self-reflexive: "What we are left with is neither territory nor map but an oscillation between them, a dialectical shadow play of presence and absence. Echoes and quotations surface briefly and are reabsorbed. . . . A series of 'first persons' is projected and erased. The speaker is not only masked but destabilized as a reference point. . . . What these voices or tones share is a deflection, either minute or broad, from their apparent contextual function. . . . The set of possible narratives, suggested withdrawn, reproposed, exists at the margin or periphery of the text."

Exists at the margin or periphery of the text.

An advance review of *First Figure* (1984), *Publishers Weekly:* "Palmer is excruciating to follow, lacking as he does even the

153

slightest pretense to logic or reality. His writing makes the excesses of the *nouveau roman* look like child's play. His gift for language is patent and undeniable, but the audience for this sort of poetry is small." What does the *PW* reviewer mean by "logic" or, especially, "reality"? Has anyone been troubled seriously by the "excesses" of the *nouveau roman* for at least twenty years? Isn't the audience for any poetry in America always really rather small?

(An anonymous reviewer of R. Barthes' *Le degré zéro de l'écriture* in *Bulletin critique du livre français,* 1953: "The real problem posed by this little book is that of finding who is going to be helped by such deliberately obscure pages, in which the ideas constantly hide themselves away behind an exaggerated, grandiloquent, metaphorical and wholly illogical mode of expression.")

Responding to the *PW* review in his New Mexico interview in 1985: "There is an Anglo-American empirical tradition that takes as a model a kind of simple version of reference, where a poem is a place in which you tell a little story, the conclusion of which is at the bottom of the poem just where it is supposed to be. . . . It doesn't admit that the question of language is a continually open one."

Is it chance, given his area of inquiry, that Palmer's first full-length collection (*Blake's Newton,* 1972) opens with a meditation on form? "Its form, at tables by fours / leap . . . relieved of their weight."

Palmer (b. 1943, NYC; lived since 1969 in SF) does not consider himself a Language poet per se, most probably because he wishes to mute the interest in theory that the term implies, at least when used in connection with Silliman (*The New Sentence*), Watten (*Total Syntax*), and Bernstein (*Content's Dream*).

Yet at every turn these poems call to mind the questionings of the Language project. "The Theory of the Flower":

> The film is of a night garden
> There is nothing meaningful about the text
> There is nothing meaningful about a text
> She
> brushed away the sand
> She brushed away the hand
> This is Paradise, an unpunctuated book
> and this is a sequence of laws
> in which the night sky is lost
> and the flower of theory is a black spot
> upon the foxglove
> (These words have all been paid for)

In the very dismissal of the "black spot" of theory, Palmer here asks us to consider the nature of the text as what Stephen Fredman (*Poet's Prose*) calls the "endless play of subtexts," his disinterest in establishing a hierarchy of texts (later in *First Figure* he includes as "poems" "prose pieces first performed on radio"), and, especially, multi-discourse or intertextuality: "So the poem becomes a shared place among a variety of texts, without, I hope, ever becoming simply a collage."

Palmer: "I like the possibility of intertextuality. I am a reader, perhaps too much of one, and I live to some degree in the book." And thus for Palmer—as for Olson, say, or J. H. Prynne—the act of close writing becomes the act of close reading, a kind of translation, a *reinscription*.

Christopher Norris (*Derrida*): "The dismantling of conceptual oppositions, the taking apart of hierarchical systems of thought which can then be reinscribed within a different order of textual signification," thus the necessity for what Derrida calls a "prudent, differentiated, slow, stratified" reading in *Dis-*

semination. "It is enough (he argues) to disqualify any reading that would confine its attentions to 'philosophy' or 'literature' and seek to close off all contaminating influences from outside its own-subject domain. Writing, in short, is intertextual through and through."

Derrida does not seem to be a figure of explicit importance for Palmer, yet when Derrida speaks of *différence* he might well be speaking of a primary aspect of Palmer's technique. Discussing the question of signification, Derrida offers the neologism "différence," meaning at least in part, *deferral:* "it expresses the interposition of delay, the interval of a spacing and temporalizing that puts off until 'later' what is presently denied, the possible that is presently impossible" ("Différence"). The sign thus becomes a kind of "differed presence"—provisional and de-centered. Hence, *Notes for Echo Lake* (notes both as musical text and, importantly, provisional/problematic draft [Pound's *Drafts & Fragments*]), an argument, at the very least, against the possibility of closure; provisional, decentered, hovering on the margin. "Alogon": "I recognise nothing from before. This might or might not have been hers. All over the world they flower at once. That's mint and lemon that you smell. He cannot seem to recall. Open or opening to a page. / She draws the remains of a recognisable face."

De-centered, *not* centerless. Derrida: "I didn't say there was no center, that we could get along without the center. I believe that the center is a function, not a being—a reality, but a function." And, importantly, "I don't destroy the subject; I situate it" (*The Structuralist Controversy*). While Palmer has little interest in personality ("that's just this guy . . ."), he recognizes the importance of the situated self, "a self that is transformed through language" (NM interview).

The poem as a kind of ongoing notebook. Of his own "notebooks," Palmer writes, "As a reader and writer outside the academy I have the luxury of wandering quasi-randomly among fields of interest—linguistics, language philosophy, musical and mathematical theory, detective novels, nature writing, psychology, and so on. My notebooks display this scatter. They are a congeries of quotations, source material, reflections and incohate writings, a kind of thief's journal or maybe more accurately, a game of blind man's bluff played among ghosts."

For a time, P. edited *Joglars* with Clark Coolidge. It is interesting to see how each has moved from rather minimalist early work of *Space* and *Blake's Newton* to such fully realized texts of the last decade as *Solution Passage* and *Notes for Echo Lake*. Of Coolidge's *Ing* and *Space,* Palmer observes (reviewing *Mine, Sulfur,* 8), "The earliest morphemic topologies function as elemental testings of an alternative perceptual order." As of Ashbery, again self-reflexively: "Words are isolated, fragmented, partially erased. Some pages read as the remains of a lost text, others as tentative disruptions of an underlying silence." From Palmer's "Without Music 2" (far less disruptive, yet illustrative):

> Controlling the light
> Controlling the flow of light
> we would meet if
> with one's blessings if
> The Cafe Lithuania is near enough
> is fairly near, is nearby if
> and the logorrheic heart
> this is partly in quotes
> and the pyrotropic heart
> like a cigarette
> when you find a blue disk

or imported toy railroad car
private, containing famous baritone
who's rich, who's very almost rich
who's here to sing if
without music even if
who's rich

Who's here to sing if. Palmer regards early Coolidge as without speaker, tone, story, and here, of course, we find all three (and certainly even in Coolidge's "these / ing / those" there are, contra-Palmer, all three, though each is far more muted than in our traditional sense of them; there is, for example, a "speaker," though, as in later Beckett, a decentered one). "All call for a determinedly participatory reading to yield their levels of referential signification."

Palmer and Coolidge share an interest in Abstract Expressionism; New Mexico interviews:

Coolidge: "I came out of a situation in the fifties where the things that were going on were Abstract Expressionist painting. . . ."

Palmer: "[de Kooning] was a painter I respected very much because he combined a quality of complexity with immediacy, and I learned a great deal from Abstract Expressionists in that sense."

For Palmer, de Kooning's technique draws particular attention: "erasing, adding on, until the figure had emerged and the work seemed complete." H. Rosenberg points out that for de Kooning the logic of the work "lies not in its rational consistency" but in the ongoing struggle with the possibilities of the medium itself; "there is no ultimate fact of which it can be the equivalent" (*The Anxious Object*). A decentered painting, a decentered poetry, in which, as in the later Wittgenstein of the

Philosophical Investigations, their languages (paint, words) do not name objects but rather take on the status of objects.

(Frank O'Hara of de Kooning: "Then he told me how he had always been interesed in mattresses because they were pulled together at certain points and puffed out at others, 'like the earth' " [*Collected Poems*].)

November 7, 1985. The San Jose Ezra Pound Conference. Arrived with Tarn . . . this morning speaking on the keynote panel with Robert Duncan and Jack Gilbert, I sit for two hours next to Duncan. He is pale, a little emaciated, obviously physically weak from his kidney illness. Just as obvious is the animation of his mind, his monologue as inclusively energetic and inner directed—in some strange way even more so—as ever. Palmer, who has become a close friend of Duncan's, is in the audience. Duncan's philosophical source is Whitehead; Palmer's, Wittgenstein.

Later, at another session, Palmer introducing his remarks on E.P. and nineteenth-century French literature with: "I happened to be reading the *Philosophical Investigations.* It's a book I've always enjoyed, and I decided this summer that I'd read it the way I like to read philosophy, as a novel. It thus opened itself out again for me; it has that same depth of linguistic resonance that you find in great books, so that the passages renew themselves. They become almost a book of your own hours in a very interesting and sympathetic way."

Palmer, at least as far as I've been able to discover, hasn't remarked on Derrida, de Man, deconstruction. Rather, his central figure is Wittgenstein: "I went to philosophy at one point looking for textures which had not been admitted into poetry. In particular, that curious rigor and beauty of Wittgenstein's sensibility gave me textures that I very much wanted to have in the poem" (NM interview). And: "Isn't part of my attraction to L.W. that he has eliminated those things I (once?) wanted eliminated from 'prose fiction': character, description, and . . . fiction? Might not Beckett be considered closer to L.W. than to most prose writers of this century?" (Notebooks, November 12, 1977).

(Coolidge also sees Beckett as a crucial source. While here he spoke of having just finished teaching a seminar at Naropa on Beckett, with focus on *The Unnamable:* "there is an incredible pronoun shift that goes on continually—he's thinking of himself, voices tell him things, he sees himself talking to himself, amazingly reflective.")

Wittgenstein offers a model of the notational, a methodology which proceeds through proposition, each unit proposing a modification of the preceding—adding, erasing, decentering. Palmer: "The notion for example of composition with nothing at its center—with *nothing* at its center." And thus, as in P.'s description of seeing Cézanne's later work at MOMA, it is all part of a single larger project, "that is, one could enter at any point and fill the entire span of attention" (Notebooks, December 5, 1977). Or John Cage on Cage: "The early works have beginnings, middles, endings. The later ones do not. They begin anywhere, last any length of time" (*Silence,* 1961).

Palmer is far more open (far more field-oriented), in the manner of Duncan, than a poet like Ashbery who, while on his own terms is hardly conventional, yet in a sense is rather conservative in terms of structure—i.e., each poem more or less remains self-referential, a closed and separate system. (Palmer himself, in the Ashbery review, disagrees with this; admitting that "the new book's shape emphasizes closure," he yet feels that in the

main "semantically the work remains in varying degrees inde-
terminate or open.") In my reading, Palmer follows in the wake
of Olson, say, via Duncan; Ashbery in the wake of Stevens.
"The unity of the *Maximus* is perhaps best compared to the
unity of a zoological species: it is an unchanging form that
perpetually reconstructs itself in useful and unexpected ways"
(Don Byrd, *Charles Olson's Maximus*).

"I was reading in the *Philosophical Investigations*," Wittgenstein's
late (1953, published posthumously) study. Offers a repudiation of "picture theory" ("a picture is a model of reality") of the
Tractatus (1921) in favor of the notion of the existence of infinite
"language-games." Early Wittgenstein argues that all propositions about a particular incident must have the same underlying
logical form, and it is through this form that we come to
understand the logical structure of the world; in the later work
he gives up the idea of "correct form," arguing instead that
sentences do far more than simply depict facts, and thus propositions are not correct or incorrect but rather understood or not
understood.

(*Publisher's Weekly:* " . . . lacking as he does even the slightest
pretense to logic or reality." Wittgenstein: "On the one hand, it
is clear that every sentence in our language is 'in order as it is.'
That is to say, we are not striving after an ideal, as if our
ordinary vague sentences had not yet got a quite unexceptional
sense, and a perfect language awaited construction by us.—On
the other hand, it seems clear that where there is sense there
must be perfect order.—So there must be perfect order even in
the vaguest sentence" [*Philosophical Investigations*].)

Stanley Cavell suggests reading *Notes for Echo Lake* as propositions. As method, this refers back to the *Tractatus*. Gr. *Satz*=

proposition/sentence, yet specifically an indicative sentence able to stand on its own with respect to its meaning. Following Aristotle (*De interpretatione*), W. proposes that "the aim of [*Tractatus*] is to set a limit to thought—or rather, not to thought, but to the expression of thought."

An early explicit reference to Wittgenstein, the series "The Brown Book" and "The Book Against Understanding" in *The Circular Gates* (1974). W.'s *Blue Book* and *Brown Book* collect preliminary studies for the *Philosophical Investigations* (i.e., dictated to his Cambridge students in the thirties). *The Brown Book,* especially, deals with the problem of language games: "I simply set forth the games as what they are, and let them shed their light on the particular problems" (LW); "To learn what to say to unlearn· / The order of islands here / The number of fingers" (MP). Following Augustine, W. argues that simply because we can speak and understand a particular language doesn't mean that we can *say* what that language means; "understanding" is as various as language games themselves. "Systems of communication we shall call 'language games.' They are more or less akin to what in ordinary language we call games. Children are taught in their native language by means of such games. . . . We are not, however, regarding the language games which we describe as incomplete parts of a language, but as languages complete in themselves, as complete systems of human understanding" (*Brown Book*).

The poem, then, as yet another language game, which may (Frost, Kinnell) or may not (Stein, Palmer) have reference to "ordinary language," and which even as "native speakers" we may or may not understand. "The Book Against Understanding," as if conscious mitigation against "ordinary understanding," which does not mean, of course, that we do not/cannot understand. A kind of mathematics.

Palmer's "mathematics": *Plan of the City of O* (1971); *Blake's Newton* (1972); *C's Songs* (1973); *Six Poems* (1973); *The Circular Gates* (1974); *Without Music* (1977); *Transparency of the Mirror* (1980); *Alogon* (1980); *Notes for Echo Lake* (1981); *First Figure* (1984); *Sun* (1988). Trans. from Rimbaud (1980) and Huidobro (1981). Ed., *Code of Signals: Recent Writings in Poetics* (1983).

Palmer: "Trying to get at the untellable story, in a way."

> This is a room.
> Give me this and
> this. This
> book ends some
> time when it ends and
> this is a room

2. Silliman and Language Poetry

(Palmer, in his NM interview: "My relation to the Language poets is this: First there is a certain disservice that's been performed, partly by themselves, in grouping a fairly diverse community of writers under that rubric for the sake of self-presentation. They came along at a certain point and were generous toward work such as mine and Clark Coolidge's. Part of that had to do with a degree of common interest, an attempt to bring into question surfaces of language, normative syntax, and so on. . . . [However,] I would say that the way I inhabit language, or language inhabits me, is in a sense more traditional than the way through procedural models that many of the so-called Language poets work.")

Language poetry. Stephen Fredman sees the writers who gather under the Language umbrella as generally privileging the critical intelligence over "the orphic, bardic impulse in American poetry" (i.e., Everson, Ginsberg; *Poet's Prose*). Of West Coast

writers like Palmer, Ron Silliman, Michael Davidson, Lyn Hejinian, and Barrett Watten, and easterners like Charles Bernstein,
Bruce Andrews, and Susan Howe: "Critical thinking does not
merely buttress the mythopoeic imagination"; rather, these poets are "originally critical, practicing a vigilant self-awareness
that calls forth language and subjects it to an examination of its
mediatory function. For these poets the critical activity of deconstruction, of investigating a text as an endless play of subtexts, is a means of poetic creation."

A genealogy: Silliman, in his preface to the anthology *In
The American Tree* (1986), takes Robert Grenier's "I HATE
SPEECH" in the first issue of *This* (co-edited with Watten,
winter 1971) to be an opening stroke. Probably first use of the
term *Language poets* as applied to this group in Silliman's anthology of poems of Andrews, Coolidge, Grenier, himself, and
others (*Alcheringa*, 1975). His preface: figures "whose work
might be said to 'cluster' about such magazines as *This, Big
Deal, Tottel's*. . . . Called variously 'language centered,' 'mini-
mal,' 'nonreferential formalism,' 'diminished referentiality,'
'structuralist.' Not a group but a tendency in the work of
many."

1977: term appears again in a special feature in *Open Letter*
(Canada, guest edited by Steve McCaffery).

Formalized to a certain degree with the appearance of
$L=A=N=G=U=A=G=E$, ed. by Andrews and Bernstein
(*The $L=A=N=G=U=A=G=E$ Book* retrospective anthology, 1984); first number February 1979, and over four years
twelve issues, two supplements, book-length final issue with
Open Letter. Lead article (Larry Eigner, "Approaching things /
Some calculus / How figure it / Of Everyday Life Experience")
sets the tone: "No really perfect optimum mix, anyway among
some thousands or many of distinctive or distinguishable things

(while according to your capacity some minutes, days or hours 2, 4, or 6 people, say, are company rather than crowds), and for instance you can try too hard or too little." Devoted to poetics, certain names appear frequently: Bernstein, Andrews, Watten, Hejinian, Silliman; topics range from signification, sound, and schizophrenia to analyses of work by Gertrude Stein, Laura (Riding) Jackson, and Louis Zukofsky. "A spectrum of writing that places its attention primarily on language and ways of making meaning, that takes for granted neither vocabulary, grammar, process, shape, syntax, program, or subject matter." Further, to generate discussion on the relation of writing to politics" to the end of producing "an analysis of the capitalist social order as a whole and of the place that alternative forms of writing and reading might occupy in its transformation" (Andrews/Bernstein, *L Book*).

The margin or periphery of the text.

LP as a critique of the prevailing aesthetic, the "workshop poem." Bob Perelman's lecture "The First Person" refers to William Stafford's "Travelling Through the Dark" as example: "Travelling through the dark I found a deer /dead on the edge of the Wilson Road. / . . . I thought hard for us all—my only swerving— / then pushed her over the edge into the river." Perelman sees this as a "voice" poem—"William Stafford has 'found his voice.'" (I spent a decade teaching creative-writing students to "find their voice"; an anthology-text, *The Voice That Is Great Within Us*.) "It's all realistic, but all it leads up to is the pathetic fallacy of '*I* could hear the wilderness listen.' A typical neo-academic dirge for nature. The poet is firmly in the driver's seat, '*I* could hear the wilderness,' and firmly in control of all the meaning, '*I* thought hard for us all.' . . . Here, the I is in a privileged position unaffected by the words" (*Hills*, 6/7).

Marjorie Perloff (*The Dance of the Intellect*) quotes Bernstein: "It's a mistake, I think, to posit the self as the primary organizing feature of writing. As many others have pointed out, a poem exists in a matrix of social and historical relations that are more significant to the formation of an individual text than any personal qualities of the life or voice of an author." Perloff employs Perelman's strategy, using as text Galway Kinnell's "Memory of Wilmington": "Thirty-some years ago, hitchhiking / north on Route 1, I stopped for the night. . . . " A random issue of *American Poetry Review* offers stances similar to Stafford/Kinnell: "The child coughs all night; / I give her orange syrup / that sticks to her hair" (Brenda Hillman); "I have watched / Everywhere / The unregarded / Holding out / Their empty tins of justice" (Howard Moss); "I learned to type ninety words a minute. / I quit the band because I wasn't stupid. / At concerts no one sat next to me" (Laurie Henry). Like poem after poem in *The New Yorker, The Nation, Ploughshares,* and *The Iowa Review,* these all share a Wordsworthian sense of the poem's task—to recall through a centered self a fixed moment. (Ashbery, on the other hand, "I wrote about what I didn't see. The experience that eluded me somehow intrigued me more than the one I was having, and this has happened to me down through the years," *SF Review of Books,* 1977). Perloff: Here the "experience is prior to the language that communicates it: the story of [Kinnell's] hobo exists in a mental realm waiting to be activated by the words of a poet who can somehow match signifier to signified." The "workshop poem" exists, that is, to convey from writer to reader an experience.

As Barthes remarks, "All modes of writing have in common the fact of being 'closed' and thus different from spoken language. Writing is in no way an instrument for communication" (*Writing Degree Zero*).

Formalism: Palmer, Silliman, Bernstein have all mentioned an interest in Russian Formalism; Watten has written an extended "talk" ("Russian Formalism and the Present," *Total Syntax*). For the Formalists language itself is the subject of poetry— "What is at stake are not the methods of literary study but the principles upon which literary science should be constructed" (Boris Ejchenbaum, 1924). Watten's talk mentions two groups: the Moscow Linguistic Circle (Roman Jakobson and Osip Brik; linguistic focus), influenced by Saussure; OPOYAZ (Society for the Study of Poetic Language; Viktor Shklovsky, Boris Eichenbaum, literary theory). A primary tenet: as in Wittgenstein, unlike "ordinary" language, "poetic" language need not necessarily correspond to the object. Jackobson: "The function of poetry is to point out that the sign is not identical with its referent."

Aaron Shurin reminds us that among poets an interest in an expanded image of the self is not recent. "A Thing Unto Myself: The unRomantic Self and Gender in the Third Person" traces the "fracturing of the complacency of first person discourse" in both Whitman and Dickinson, finding in Rimbaud especially a model for the projection of the "self into the realm of what Emile Benveniste calls the non or third person, whose indication is not presence but absence" (*Code of Signals,* Palmer, ed.). Palmer: "If only a self got posited in a poem we may as well be having lunch somewhere and not bothering with poems" (NM interview).

Ron Silliman: "A lesson I've learned from a year's work in the Tenderloin . . . is that psychotics & most street alcoholics respect an aggressive *assertion of presence*" (*The Poetry Reading,* Vincent/Zweig, eds.).

Whose indication is not presence but absence. Derrida's "The Supplement of Origin": "The total absence of the subject and object of a statement—the death of the writer and/or the disappearance of the objects he was able to describe—does not prevent a text from 'meaning' something. On the contrary, this possibility gives birth to meaning as such."

Ron Silliman (ed. *Socialist Review;* born 1946, Pasco, Washington; removed early to Berkeley, then SF) offers, most cogently, the political dimension: "We do not contain multitudes so much as we are the consequence of a multitude of conflicting and overdetermined social forces, brought to us, and acted out within us, as language" ("Realism").

(Almost a third of Andrews/Bernstein anthology is devoted to "Writing and Politics"; the critique is leftist [with recurrent references to Marx, Althusser, Jameson] with pieces ranging from "Writing Social Work and Political Practice" [Andrews] and "The Dollar Value of Poetry" [Bernstein] to "Writing and Capitalism" [Watten] and "Capitalistic Useless Phrases after Endless" [Hannah Weiner].)

Silliman stresses the question of the poem as "commodity." "Disappearance of the Word, Appearance of the World" (*The New Sentence*) opens with epigraphs from Sapir and Marx, recalling that we are all in a real sense products of the language which inhabits us (Palmer: "language inhabits me") and, further, that the material world conditions our consciousness. Attempting what he calls Louis Zukofsky's "projection of a possible 'scientific' definition of poetry," he outlines three elements of the question (Perloff, "the classic Marxist position"): "(1) the stage of historical development determines the natural laws (or, if you prefer the terminology, the underlying structures) of poetry; (2) the stage of historical development determines the natural laws of language; (3) the primary impact on language, and language arts, of the rise of capitalism has been in the area of reference and is directly related to the phenomena known as the commodity fetish."

Two types of human relationships—the group and the series. Tribal societies retain "the expressive integrity of the gestural nature of language," and this accounts for our general inability to deal with such language as anything other than "nonsense." (Wittgenstein: "Don't *for heaven's* sake, be afraid of talking nonsense! But you must pay attention to your nonsense.") Capitalist "serialization," however, "places the individual as a passive cipher into a series of more or less identical units," as, finally, "the function of commoditized tongue of capitalism" becomes "the serialization of the language-user, especially the reader." Importantly, "what happens when a language moves toward and passes into a capitalist stage of development is an anaesthetic transformation of the perceived tangibility of the word, with corresponding increases in its descriptive and narrative capacities, preconditions for the invention of 'realism,' the optical illusion of reality in capitalist thought." These developments, Silliman concludes, under capitalism "deform" reference into referentiality.

(Sven Birkerts, on Ashbery, negatively: "For me, verbal reference and linguistic structure are fundamental elements in the rule system of a game called meaning. It is a game—I see that—but by my lights it's the only game in town. . . . [Ashbery's poetry] will prove to have been a dead-end—interesting, at times beguiling, ultimately nihilistic" [*Sulfur* 19]. Responses, same issue, by Eliot Weinberger, Coolidge, Palmer, Jed Rasula. Or Alain Robbe-Grillet, who argues that any new form "will always seem more or less an absence of any form at all, since it is unconsciously judged by reference to the consecrated forms" ["A Future for the Novel"]. Hence, E.P.'s thirty-year time lag.)

"Commodity fetish." In *Das Capital,* Marx speaks of the "fetishism of the commodity." William C. Dowling (*Jameson, Althusser, Marx*): prior to the existence of a "market," there is no mention of "market value," only "use value"—"the value that an object or product has when I have transformed it from its raw materials through my own labor." Once a market economy is in place, however, once we become members "of a society where even a rudimentary division of social labor is carried out," the whole foundation of our thought changes. Once we begin to exchange commodities on a basis that is other than use value, we are participating in "an illusion called market value; it really is the market, as an impersonal system assigning commodities their worth within a system of exchange, that has begun to determine value now." This new value "divorces the worth of objects from the labor that went into their creation and the use to which they may rationally be put, and therefore estranges humanity from itself." It is Althusser's contribution, Dowling concludes, to sense that ideology is the key—"economic systems in general and capitalism in particular work to conceal their essential operations while presenting to those who inhabit them an illusory appearance of things."

Silliman ("The Political Economy of Poetry," *The New Sentence*) quotes Laura (Riding) Jackson's complaint in her essay (1926) "T. E. Hulme, the New Barbarism, and Gertrude Stein," concerning "the forced professionalization of poetry," a complaint which has at its base a revulsion at a sense of poetry as commodity rather than simply product (market value rather than use value). Reference to Daniel Halpern's *American Poetry Anthology* (the apotheosis of the "workshop poem") as a prime example of poetry as capitalist commodity. (While large trade publishers produce less than 5 percent of all poetry titles, over 50 percent of the poets included in Halpern are derived from this material.)

Or: *American Poetry Review*—photographs of poets, ads for books, conferences, journals, and self-perpetuating writing programs. The prevalence of the photographs is especially interesting in light of the participation of the workshop poem in the "optical illusion" of the first person, as if the editors go so far as to distrust even the *I* of the poem and so must reinforce the false realism by having "real" people staring back at the reader.

(Eliot Weinberger makes a number of similar points, especially about "the workshop poem," in his scathing review of Carolyn Forche's *The Country Between Us* [*Sulfur* 6]: "There is the book's cover: a photograph of what might be Hugh Hefner's last girlfriend. It is, of course, the author herself, in misty Extreme Close Up, with head tilted up, eyes looking dreamily toward the light, full lips slightly parted. Why would Forche, a leftist and a feminist, allow herself [possibly choose] to be marketed in this manner?")

S.'s "Disappearance": "By recognizing itself as the *philosophy of practice in language,* poetry can work to search out the preconditions of post-referential language within the existing social fact. This requires (1) recognition of the historic nature and struggle of referentiality, (2) placing the issue of language, the repressed element, at the center of the program, and (3) placing the program into the context of conscious class struggle." The workshop poem, with its insistence on translatable experience, fails to question the historical, social, and economic context, merely accepting as given the prevailing "market value." It refuses to recognize (Bernstein, "The Dollar Value of Poetry") that "we speak of poetry as being untranslatable and unparaphrasable, for what is untranslatable is the sum of all the specific conditions of the experience (place, time, order, light, mood, position to infinity) made available by reading." And it is for this reason that many of the LP's insist on a poetry which resists any "normative standardization in the ordering of words in the unit or the sequencing of these units"; resists, that is, the *APR* poem.

Perloff on Amy Clampitt's *Imago:* "Everything here will yield to 'translation' provided one uses one's dictionary and encyclopedia. Given this emphasis on translatability, I take the Amy Clampitt cult as a sign of our current nostalgia for the good gone days when POETRY WAS ABOUT SOMETHING" (*Sulfur*, 10).

Referentiality. It is not that poems are thoroughly "nonreferential," or can be. Jackson MacLow takes issues with "practioners and sympathetic critics" whom (he says) posit nonreferentiality: "All signs point to what they signify. All signs have significance." Silliman says flatly, "Words are not, finally, nonreferential. For they originate in interactions with the world" ("Disappearance"). Palmer agrees: "I'm not interested in making poetry if I cannot explore the areas of signification that are less available in other areas of discourse. I want language to signify and be functional, and in that respect I have to investigate all aspects of the non-logical and the discontinuous" (NM interview).

Creeley: "Poems are not referential, or at least importantly so," and along this line the LP's seek simply to diminish the importance of reference. Silliman: "By the creation of non-referring structures (Coolidge, Di Palma, Andrews), disrupting of context (Grenier, DeJasu), forcing the meanings in upon themselves until they cancel out or melt (Watten, the poem *Tri,* and, elsewhere, in the work of Michael Palmer). By effacing one or more elements of referential language (a tactic commonly employed by the Russian Futurists), the balance within the word shifts, redistributes" ("Disappearance").

"Not 'death' of the referent—rather a recharged use of the multivalent referential vectors that any word has" (Bernstein, "Thought's Measure"). The issue is not, again, reference per se, but a reaction to a prevailing poetics which seems to be unaware of the social implications which hover just outside its acceptance as a first given an unquestioning referentiality.

The *text* as *text,* opposed to (Snyder, Rothenberg) a sense of text as (finally) a *score* for oral performance—i.e., a kind of substitute of an absent oral tradition. (Ron Sukenick: "Did you ever attend a Gary Snyder reading, with three quarters of the audience applauding in the wrong places? If living performance is the thing, what happens after the poet has died?" "Against Readings.") The nature of the text is problematic; there is little interest in establishing a hierarchy of modes or even distinguishing between prose and poetry (or fiction from anthropology from automobile repair guides).

Bernstein (*Paris Review*): "There is a willingness to use, within the space of a text, a multiplicity of such different modes, which counts more on a recognition of the plastic qualities of traditional genres and styles than on their banishment." Thus, Stein's *Tender Buttons,* Williams's *Kora in Hell* as models for "poet's prose": Ashbery's *Three Poems,* Silliman's *Tjanting* and *Ketjak,* Hejinian's *My Life,* Rodefer's *Four Lectures.*

Stein (via Silliman): "To please a young man there should be sentences. What are sentences. Like what are sentences. In the part of sentences it for him is happily all. They will name sentences for him. Sentences are called sentences."

8 ✺ The Place of Poetry in the West: A Conversation with William Everson and Nathaniel Tarn

Originally intended as a "Poets on Poetry" conversation for American Poetry, *the following discussion took place at William Everson's home in the Santa Cruz Mountains on June 3, 1986. Though Everson and Nathaniel Tarn had followed one another's work for many years, and had recently begun a correspondence, this occasion marked their first meeting.*

Nathaniel Tarn: I'm very interested in the whole question of whether there is, or is not, an "American poetic language" or "American idiom." From Williams on, this has been an important question, though it seems now to be stopped short by the internationalism of a present scene everyone is concerned about, the "Language" community of poetry.

Lee Bartlett: Bill, have you thought much about the Language poets? Ron Silliman? Barrett Watten? Bruce Andrews? Charles Bernstein?

William Everson: The names of those particular writers are familiar to me, but I've never gotten into any of their theoretical writing. *Language poets* is an entirely new term to me.

Tarn: Well, I wonder if it's even still a live question, "Language" poets aside. The question of an American poetic language.

Everson: For me it is. In fact, I'm just getting into it as I write my long autobiographical epic. I find myself resorting to slang, idiomatic expressions that I never would have allowed into my more formal verse. It's as if I'm in a new place, more secular, letting my secular side have a voice. So now I find myself inhabiting the American idiom in a way I never thought necessary for me.

Tarn: But that is a personal thing. What does it mean in terms of the overall scene? Is this still a live issue in the culture at large?

Everson: I don't think it can be avoided. I think it's going to be around as long as America has any kind of place in the world of thought and letters. We are, after all, infecting the purity of all other idioms on the earth through our media.

Bartlett: Although interestingly Helen Vendler has a new anthology called *The Harvard Book of Contemporary American Poetry,* which begins with Stevens, yet includes no Pound, Williams, Oppen, H.D., all the way up through no Duncan or Creeley. It's as if for Vendler and Harvard there is a very narrow and peculiar American idiom. Kenneth Rexroth regarded Williams the greatest American prosodist of this century. Can you imagine an anthology of American poetry published in 1986 which includes Stevens but not Williams?

Everson: Only for a special purpose. Maybe tracking a trend.

Bartlett: Yet she includes Ginsberg and Snyder. I can't see either of them coming out of Stevens.

Everson: No, neither can I. Stevens was the Matisse of American poetry.

Bartlett: Nathaniel, you represent an interesting case in this context. Born in Paris, raised and educated more or less in England, and yet you consider yourself now an American poet. Obviously for you the question of an American idiom must be an open one.

Tarn: Well, I try to listen in that way. I am coming, by listening, into speaking that way also. I suppose that, to a certain extent, this involves a theatrical component. It is linguistic *work*. Poets are linguistic *workers*. Actors, for instance, spend a great deal of time perfecting their idioms. I could have gone, I suppose, to an elocution school, except that there is something inauthentic about that. When I die, the telltale voice will have died with me.

Bartlett: But you and Bill both seem to be thinking of idiom as lexical—que over against line, for example. I'm thinking of it more as, say, cadence.

Tarn: It's both. I *certainly* do not think of it as lexical only.

Everson: I found Nathaniel's *At the Western Gates* quite American in idiom, and I was very impressed by that. His asking how in the hell do you go about fucking here, in a cabin at the end of the continent.

Tarn: When I arrived in America in the late sixties and very early seventies, I was tremendously hopeful because so many of the ethnic voices were coming on strong. It was a linguistic progress that in some ways reminded me of what had happened in England following the war. Although the standard BBC voice had dominated as long as you could remember, after the war, provincial voices came in, so that you began to hear Liverpool, Nottingham, the Angry Young Men, particularly in the theater. England seemed to be listening to itself for the first time. I don't think America was listening to itself for the first time in the sixties and seventies—it had always been more democratic and more populist—but nevertheless it seemed to me a time in which the American language was growing in every possible direction, and the English language was not.

But now, after having lived here fifteen years, and after having gotten through fifteen years of teaching and so on, I've gotten somewhat disappointed with that, lost some of my faith in that. Now, I'm more impressed with the deadening of language which is taking place in the media and in political discourse, a kind of ironing out of the thing into a set of commercial formulae. Bill, as I think I've told you, I think you have five-hundred times more faith than anyone else I've ever met, and yet in *Birth of a Poet* you mention this problem only once or twice. You are just far more optimistic than I am. The kids are listening to that stuff more and more, and talking it, and now, instead of expanding, the language is retreating.

Everson: Well, my faith on this question is rooted in the archetype. It doesn't have much to do with these more temporal aspects of the problem. It constantly manifests itself in a primal and refreshing way which is inexhaustible; it's the root source of the language per se. My orientation point toward reality is psychological and profoundly symbolic, and for me the poetry lies in the subject matter rather than in the expression. It is the inexhaustible current in the subject of the archetype itself which is the great replenishing factor. The ordeal of the poet is in reconnecting to that, as in prayer.

Bartlett: This takes us back to the American idiom. You are saying that it's not lexical, not a cadence, but subject matter?

Everson: No. The idiom is a matter of expression. I'm not an advocate of the American idiom as Williams was. I employ it because you get vibrations of truth out of it which are relevant to where we find ourselves at any given time. But for me it's not as important as the American idiom, or the Canadian idiom, or the Australian idiom, or the British idiom. The language itself has its own inner dynamic which is the crucial factor.

Tarn: It seems to me it has to be *both* expression *and* subject matter, but that expression primes—otherwise why *poetry?* I've got a feeling that this is linked to another question, the mission or function of the poet. Bill, you have a very high regard for the poet as the conservator of language and a healer of the problems of the nations. The poet can only contact solutions through the prophetic function, the shamanistic function. Of course, Ezra Pound had this same kind of high regard for the poet, and it seems to me that one of the primary reasons he was so tragically disappointed late in his life was that his vision really was beginning to encounter the wall of silence he had not wanted to perceive before. So my question here would be rather brutal. Do you think that the coming generations are going to have all that elevated a notion of the poet? My sense of what younger poets are doing today does not imply that prophetic idea of the poet at all.

Bartlett: I'd agree with that. Certainly I think Michael Palmer would deny a prophetic vocation, as would a poet coming out of Iowa's MFA program.

Everson: Poetry goes through changes from primitivism to decadence; we happen to be in a decadent period right now. However, the mythic possibilities are always there, and they'll never be exhausted. If you get a strong enough personality you'll recover those elements. If at a particular time he or she hasn't shown up, then he or she simply hasn't shown up. You just have to wait for the voice that can tap it, and there you'll get the replenishing energy.

Bartlett: Like Yeats.

Everson: Yes, exactly. He was just late enough to be post-Victorian and early enough to be modernist. And he was able to achieve that vatic voice.

Bartlett: But Nathaniel, your sense of the poet is in some sense similar to Bill's.

Tarn: Well, one of the problems I have had for a while is the nightmare of an incestuous circle: that the consumers of poetry are the producers of poetry and that there is nothing else. It's a self-reinforcing circle in the sense that if none of the poets want that notion of function, then none of the readers will because they are, after all, the poets. I think we have to rediscover the reader, the function in the system of the reader as "other." Without "other" there is no *marriage*. Only incest.

Everson: The problem lies in the fact that we are in a new phase of the media and the poets are confused right now among the influx of various alien sources. It's again a matter of waiting for a strong enough voice to emerge in the recovery of taproots. As Emerson insists, if we live in expectation it will happen.

Bartlett: Although it is always possible that American poetry is finished. It's possible that we've lived through a couple hundred years of a great literature, a great poetry, and now it has worked itself out. Maybe next time it'll emerge in Bangkok, a whole other tradition.

Tarn: I doubt that, but at the same I find it hard in the face of all the sociological evidence to have Bill's faith that at some point the voice is going to reemerge. After all, in purely sociological terms, the voice that may be most *listened* to at this moment—a very uneven voice, but the most listened to—is probably somebody like Allen Ginsberg. Does he have this idea?

Everson: The oracular incentive. But nobody reads him much these days.

Bartlett: I don't think Ginsberg is all that popular now. I think that somebody like John Ashbery is far more popular at the moment, at least among people who pay attention in any sustained way to poetry. On the other hand, a poet like Galway Kinnell . . . he read not too long ago in a very large room at the University of New Mexico and we had a standing-room-only crowd. And he's got something close to the religious sense of the poet.

Everson: Well, he's a fresh voice for the neoacademics. He's got that traditional dimension which Ginsberg lacks. Ginsberg's idiom is so much looser than Kinnell's. I am not saying that Kinnell is a better poet, not in the ultimate sense of the vocation, for at his top Ginsberg is inimitable. But you can see how new academics would espouse Kinnell—he brings along with him something from the traditional canon.

Bartlett: Very simply, he writes poems that are in some sense easier to teach in the classroom. There is not all that much you can say about a Ginsberg poem after a certain point. But getting back to your observation, Bill, it's like this voice that's hovering out there waiting to be embodied is the tongue of the race. It doesn't really matter whether it's expressed in 1985 or fifty years from now.

Everson: That's my point, though I do take it on faith. It's always happened that way though. Here I am seventy-three years old and I feel it stirring in myself, glowing and burning, whispering, imploring, pleading.

Bartlett: But as an anthropologist Nathaniel would be forced to see this as a wonderful romantic fiction.

Tarn: Yes, as an anthropologist I'd have to see it that way, but as a poet—well, there is that terrible division again which I've suffered through all my life. I am a little uneasy about this conversation, playing devil's advocate again. Poets are hard on science—*need* it from Pound to Cage down to now, yet always dump on it. Actually, I'd have a faith at two removes. I'd have the faith that Bill's faith works, or I'd at least try to. But there's something else I'd like to get to. Reading through *Birth of a Poet,* I notice that you say we are passing beyond nationalism. I wish to God this were true. But as we prepare for a third world war, everyone is in the rhetorical posture of a passionate nationalism. The whole social structure of nationalism continues unabated. I don't see Albania shrinking by one jot into something that is not Albania, or the United States growing into something other. All the frontiers seem to be remaining exactly the way they are. I can see that reason and faith are asking for an end to nationalism, but it's just not happening. Look at the number of *new* nations! It is like a plague of locusts. Not that they should not be *free!* But that they should be *nations?*

Everson: Everyone knows it's over. Only the inertia of the past is carrying it on. We haven't found the new way yet, but everyone knows in their bones that it's over. We are living in a ghost, waiting for the new forms to emerge.

Tarn: I'm just not sure this is so. The poets know this, and the artists, and the environmentalists. But what about the gigantic mass of businessmen, soldiers, technicians?

Bartlett: I see us as transforming nationalism into something else, but the impulse is the same. Transformation into a re-ligious zeal—"born-again" Christians, for example, who tend to huddle under an American umbrella, but who are obviously Christians before they are Americans, when they can make such a distinction at all. Or corporate executives who'd love to merge Ford with Toyota, so that their sense of nationalism is an overarching corporation. You don't necessarily have national borders anymore, but interests and sympathies to which large groups of people adhere. And they are of necessity at odds with one another.

Everson: I see the widespread preoccupation with oriental religions as a great sign of the passing of nationalism.

Bartlett: But do you think that search really has filtered into the general population?

Everson: It doesn't matter. The portent is the eye of the fact-to-be. It is already here.

Bartlett: Maybe in Santa Cruz, but what about San Jose?

Everson: It's in the atmosphere. Everything is carrying us into a supranational consciousness. Our technology, the space flights.

Bartlett: But isn't this just a hypernationalism? Get our flag on the moon first?

Everson: The logo, not the cutting edge. The blade is ideology. There will always be nationalism, just as there will always be city pride. But men no longer kill and die for it as they did in the thirteenth century when the city-states supplanted the feudal hegemony, and gave us the Renaissance and Culture. With the sixteenth century came nationalism, which gave us the Enlightenment and Science, between them leveling Culture to Civilization. Now in the twentieth century comes Ideology. World War I was the last great nationalistic war, but it conceived in its violent womb the fountainhead of Ideology, the Russian Revolution, and Fascism arose to match it. True, both Germany and Russia revived nationalism in World War II, for Ideology was not yet strong enough to muster the millions, but that was a death rattle. The terrible spawn of the atomic bomb sealed its doom. The obsolete nations are terrified, shitting their britches. Reagan and Gorbachev embrace each other convulsively, invoking God or destiny that the fearful nationalistic death throes can be contained till Ideology can stop clearing its throat and do its thing. I take secularism and religion to be Ideology's Janus face. So far secularism is winning hands down for the age is linear, but with the rise of the cyclical religion begins to breathe. Look at the environmentalist movement. The call of the prenational.

Bartlett: But Bill, even there we've seen a tremendous backlash. It's true that James Watt is out, but a popular bumper sticker is "Nuke the Whales," and I think there is very little irony there. A lot of people are just tired of hearing about nuclear power plants and saving whales. I know that you don't spend any time in shopping malls, but if you did I think you'd be a little depressed.

Everson: They are just howling in the dark. The future is against them. You've got to go after the new consciousness as the wave of the future.

Tarn: Do you think wilderness is still the archetypal American experience?

Everson: The archetypal American address, the archetypal American vision, the archetypal American fantasy. And that's the thing that counts. Reality can offer very little to stand against it.

Tarn: Well, you have the running dream or ambition of the West which is never reached. It occurs to me that this is a transformed metaphor for immortality, because if you never reach the place where the sun goes down you never die. But in fact when you reach the great ocean you can't move further forward. What then happens? Does the whole thing then retract upon itself? Does it go inwards and promote some kind of sickness? I'm wondering about this because you've talked a great deal about violence, and I've never been completely clear on the relationship between reaching the sea and violence. Are you sometimes implying that the violence arises out of the fact that we have reached the last frontier?

Everson: No. I don't think that's the source of violence, though thinking about it now, maybe you are right. Maybe each generation feels threatened by this and therefore resorts to violence to restore the new. But generally I think of violence as being an aperture to primal reality, in the sense that the gash is manifestation of dynamic energy. This attempt to get at the dynamic energy that supercedes the form in an attempt to clarify the present and the nature of the future is what the impulse to violence is. I think that, after Christ, it can only have its true resolution in art, where it can be handled in the formal rather than the physical dimension. In a sense, the resort to violence on the material level is a failure of aesthetics. If the aesthetics were properly functioning, violence would transmute into another dimension and the energies could go forward. But there is always a degree of rupture in material forms in nature, which is both closing and opening as a way to the future.

Bartlett: Are you thinking of violence as personal or institutional?

Everson: I think of it as it is in nature first of all, the rupture and disparity between forms and the contingent reality in the process of evolution. The constant subsumption of one form into another. This is a problem for mankind as a spiritual being in the continuum of material forms, of which he is also a part. As a Christian I think this is met first on the cross, then in art.

Tarn: You've said Buddhism is a very fine system, but that it doesn't satisfy you because it's not dramatic enough. It doesn't account for any drama in the world.

Everson: Well, I don't know too much about it, but my intuition is that it withdraws from the point of violence. The reason I remain a Christian is the drama of the cross. For me that's the point of ultimate reality, ultimate truth. I remain a Christian rather than a Buddhist because of this sense that Buddhism is a deferral, rather than an embracing of violence.

Tarn: I'm not really sure that that is so. For instance, in the Zen school of meditation the amount of violence one has to face while sitting still—the violence of trying to remain in the relative world while striving for something else—is amazing. To use your terminology, the violence of having to live in linear time while at the same time trying to transcend it, to get into cyclical time. The amount of violence engendered in the sitting person is tremendous. This tends to be ritualized in those incredible encounters which take place in sesshin. It seems to me that there is certainly a ritual of violence in various forms of Buddhism. The fierce and angry-seeming deities in Tibetan Buddhism are channels for dealing with violence inside us and outside us. It is not just a quietism, which is what you seem to be implying with the word *deferral*.

Bartlett: But isn't the point of convergence in both Christian violence and Buddhist violence that fact that in each tradition at the moment of violence there is no past and no future, only the here and now? Violence offers the ultimate instance of existential focus.

Everson: Well, my further problem with Zen is the notion that reality is an illusion. I don't think it's an illusion at all.

Tarn: Again, the illusion thing is tricky. There's the Zen statement that when you go in, the mountains and rivers are there; then the mountains and rivers disappear; when you come out, the mountains and rivers are there once again. This seems to be implying that the question of illusion is complex, to say the least!

Everson: A psychological process in any case.

Tarn: To come back to the matter of America. I spent three long seasons in Alaska, and I was absolutely fascinated by what was going on there in terms that were usually codified into "this is the last frontier." The huge debate over "what we are going to do with the place." It is, somehow, "our last chance." I was always overwhelmed by the feeling that people wanted to get it over and done with; that they were profoundly uncomfortable with there *being* an Alaska. Alaska's position on the map is awkward. It *is* the West's culmination, a grand explosion, yet it feels north rather than west. Most times, it is "off the map": people in the "Lower Forty-eight" prefer to forget it. We had gotten to the Pacific and the book was, we thought, closed. Suddenly we discovered that there was still another state to be developed, and what do we do with the problem now that we've decided that the issue is closed? For Bill, of course, it would never close, but I still don't see how once we've reached the Pacific we can keep that question open. It loses the force of myth and becomes, say, "folklore." Is that where we want to go?

Bartlett: So your sense of this is simply as a stage in history, or at least spiritual history.

Tarn: Yes, which is why I have a problem with the notion of waiting for the "new" voice.

Everson: It's a matter of transmutation to another dimension. That's the function of the artist.

Tarn: Will violence remain in this new situation?

Everson: It will have to remain.

Bartlett: What do you mean by "another dimension"? It sounds like something out of science fiction.

Everson: I mean the spiritual, or the imaginative—some other dimension of the collective unconscious. It's waiting to be tapped.

Bartlett: So that the impulse to go west is simply a momentary manifestation in history of the larger psychological process?

Everson: If you wish. We are at a great moment, though, in that we have reached the ultimate West. That's why Alaska has a temptation about it as a last frontier, but that's not the problem. The problem is that the line is drawn at the Pacific. And that's the relevance of Jeffers. He made the first great penetration of the post-Pacific spiritual tendency. For his pantheism gave him the map.

Bartlett: The cynical answer again might be that once you've reached the West, the Pacific, the game is over. Nuclear weapons, AIDS, wholesale starvation. . . .

Everson: Those signs of impasse will confront us, all kinds of ghoulish threats.

Tarn: There is another *realpolitik* take here. We are continuing across the Pacific into Asia, which raises the whole issue of the fact that once the inner empire has been built, you move to the outer empire. And God knows that one of the crucial issues of our time is American imperialism. We tried it in Vietnam and it didn't work, though now we are continuing it in Central and South America. Of course, there is the alleged coming of the "Pacific Century." We may have lost the strength for empire by then—too much competition from Japan, Korea, China. Our West should do well though, even if only commercially.

Bartlett: Why don't you have an interest in the north/south axis? Why simply the east/west?

Everson: Because that's the sun pattern. East is life, west is death. The sun is born and the sun dies. I think of the north-south polarities as stable, fixed. They define the course through which the mobile and changing east-west equation must flow.

Tarn: One of the problems I always feel with "archetypal" situations is this: Alaska is in a sense north, but in another way it is very much the continuation of west. If you think of the Rockies as being "archetypally" western, in British Columbia you begin to reach the immense culmination of the West. In a sense, reaching the Pacific Ocean was really a mistake on the ultimacy of the West, which could be continued into the Aleutian archipelago right on to Japan. One of the things that worries me about "archetypal" thinking is that there is very frequently a slippage of categories because the archetype strives to divide the world ruthlessly into its various components. So one finds oneself saying, "Well in this respect it's the west, but in that respect it's north; in some senses it is female, but then it is also male." Symbolically, it's a glorious system, but it seems to me to sometimes negate and drown out the complexity of detail, and my more scientific side begins to rebel.

Everson: Yes, it is incorrigibly reductive, but then so are all symbols, all symbolism. All I can say is that the simplicity of the archetypes is so threatening that if it weren't for a little slippage here and there we'd be in a bad way.

Tarn: I suppose that fits with your notion of *imprecision,* which of course would drive the scientist crazy. Even when science talks of imprecision (all the way to chaos) it wishes to do it precisely.

Bartlett: But of course the American continent really stops at the Sierras, and all the coast is really part of a whole other land mass which includes Japan, the Pacific basin.

Tarn: Fifteen years or so ago, Robin Blaser had a magazine which was called *Pacific Nation,* and I've always had tremendous sympathy for that idea. One of the things I used to say which made me unpopular in the East was that America was entirely expendable until you got to the Rockies. That's probably one of the reasons I'm in New Mexico right now. I'm a western secessionist at heart. All the rest is still Europe.

Bartlett: Except that you've told me before that you're a little troubled by Bill's sense of the East Coast/West Coast literary politics scene.

Tarn: Well, I do have a question there. Bill, I was surprised when I was reading *Birth of a Poet* to see that you felt that western writers still had to go east to be recognized and blessed. I noticed to my surprise also during the Ezra Pound Conference in San Jose, where Lee and I just spoke, that during one panel Robert Duncan suddenly said that his recent National Poetry Award given by Thomas Parkinson's group was all very fine, but that it really doesn't mean anything because it's an award the West is giving to itself. So what does it mean? By that he seems to be saying that the eastern reputation business still holds. I just don't think it does, and I'm very surprised, Bill, that you and Duncan have that kind of defeatism. It's very untypical of you both.

Bartlett: But again to go back to the Vendler anthology, she includes Snyder and Roethke, but as far as I remember they are the only poets from this side of the country she chooses. That's an interesting situation in 1985. Neither Duncan nor Bill are in the book. No Charles Bukowski. Even someone like Carolyn Kizer, whom you'd otherwise expect. . . .

Everson: The accumulation of the past lies in the East. And it's on the basis of the accumulation of the past that judgments are made. This is inescapable. I just don't think that the East is going to validate the West until the transmutation process which we were discussing earlier is complete. When the Pacific Coast becomes the new East through that process, then we'll have a shift in recognition.

Tarn: I believe that demography and economics will soon allow us to recognize that the West is now the living center of the nation's cultural life. The East will have simply dropped away. But you are saying that the archetype still holds, but the West has to become the East for it to be realized?

Everson: Yes, exactly.

Tarn: That's what I would call an enormous category slippage, and unnecessary!

Everson: Isn't it that way with London? The East Coast still feels it needs validation from London. And Paris! Not to mention the lust for the Nobel Prize.

Tarn: Sure. I think of New York and the East Coast as the "British ghetto." *The New York Review of Books, The New Yorker,* and the Ivy League are the last remaing possessions of

Her Majesty's government in the country. So that the East Coast establishment—which produces a Helen Vendler or, God help us, a Harold Bloom—is still British owned. But that is, in your terms, "a ghost we are living in."

Bartlett: Why? Bill would see this, I think, as an archetypal situation, but from your point of view what is the reason for this?

Tarn: I just had a take on it this summer. I went back to England for the first time since I came to New Mexico, and it had finally stopped getting on my nerves. I began to realize that it was no longer home and that I could begin to enjoy it for the historical and traditional dimensions which it had. It's the history department of the University of the United States. But at the same time I understood why so many people loved it for the history and tradition, so that they then committed the crime of considering that that's where everything came from. It became the great model, thereby perpetually undermining American culture. Until one gets out from under all of that, simply refuses to accept those validations anymore, I don't see that the real new voices can arise.

Bartlett: But even in university English departments, where people should know better, there is always a sense of American writing as a poor stepchild. But I misunderstood, I think, something you said earlier. You weren't denying Bill's sense of an East/West division, but rather you simply couldn't understand why a western writer would care about it.

Tarn: Absolutely. Which is why I was so surprised by Duncan's statement.

Everson: But don't you see, the East holds the canon of judgment while the West holds the canon of creativity. We create out here in order to be judged back there. From the impersonal archetypal point of view, to write to the East's proscription would be fatal, a true defeat—the western writer who goes east and goes to pot, like Steinbeck. But having written one must wait for the East to catch up.

Bartlett: So that getting a Pulitzer Prize would carry more weight than the National Poetry Award.

Everson: For a Californian.

Tarn: See, I have great trouble with that. I don't see that there is any evidence that the Pulitzer ever meant a damn thing in real terms. Same as, nine times out of ten, the Nobel means very little. I cannot accept "we create out here in order to be judged back there." It's too close to slavery.

Bartlett: But don't you think in part your attitude derives from the fact that you've already got a British background and an eastern background—both of which you decided to leave behind? You do not have that almost innate sense of lack of worth the westerner takes in with mother's milk.

Tarn: Well, I could see this in terms of old, frozen Europe—say London as opposed to English provincial writers. As I said earlier, after the war the provincial writers took over London (the French are still backward in regard to Paris).

Bartlett: But that's the point. They *took over* London. Maybe they returned to the countryside, but there was obviously a feeling that they had to capture the capital. Until Bill and Duncan have captured New York—which, in both their cases, publication by New Directions in a sense effects—that transformation cannot be achieved.

Tarn: But this is still a *new* country! Bill, I feel that your adherence to the archetype theory is almost compelling you to remain in a defeatist position. If you maintain that the eastern archetype is fixed, then there is no reason why the situation of the western writer should change. But this brings me to another question. I wonder if, in your notion of the shaman, there isn't a confusion of the geographic with the ethnographic. That is to say: we have a tendency to think that the American Indian, who is the primal and prime owner of this land, is somehow the fountainhead of our own tradition because we are in the same place, the same *geography*. So that we mask an *ethnographic* imperialism, with all its attendant murders and massacres, with a geographic adhesion of son to father. We try to claim descent from these people, but they don't accept it. And the fact that they don't accept this seems to me to be absolutely cardinal. You must be familiar with the Indian reaction to Jerome Rothenberg's ethnopoetics.

Bartlett: Leslie Silko has a scathing essay on Snyder's "white shamanism."

Tarn: Yes, exactly. How do you feel about this, Bill? It seems to me that you have a much more deeply rooted view of shamanism in terms of your theoretical background than a number of these other people. I'm drawing attention to this because I think one needs to transcend the whole East/West discussion to solve it.

Everson: You speak as an anthropologist, and I respect your concern. Perhaps I do presume too much, as you say; but the truth is I place far more emphasis on the Spirit of Place. It is the numinous force that resolves the apparent confusion between what you call "the geographic and ethnographic spheres." The Spirit of Place is the power that makes the aboriginal shaman and the civilized poet two beads on the same thread. It is the power in the American earth that led me to seek the clue as to how it is properly met, and that clue proves to be the shaman. This place was here eons before the Indians arrived. Both our peoples were engendered somewhere else—his in Asia, mine in Europe. But we were drawn ineluctably by the same force; only his people have a longer tenure on it than mine. Nevertheless, any man with eyes to see, nerves to feel, can receive it. As Jeffers has said of the Greeks: "The Greeks were not the inventors / Of shining clarity and jewel-sharp form and the beauty of God. / He was free with men before the Greeks came: / He is here naked on the shining water. / Every eye that has a man's nerves behind it has known it." As for the shaman, were I to usurp his cult, imitate his rites and practices, he would clearly have the right to object, especially if I had not been received into the tribe, initiated into the mysteries, validated by the elders. It would be as presumptuous and futile as trying to consecrate the eucharist in the Mass without ordination. Poets are sometimes called priests of the world, prophets. But this has become a cliché. It is the shaman's penetration of the unconscious to engage the demonic that causes the poet to turn to him for a model. It is not a case of either Snyder or myself trying to pass ourselves off as bona fide shamans.

Bartlett: So you don't see this as a question of cultural imperialism?

Everson: No, though obviously there are traces of it. Maybe it is cultural imperialism in inception, but it can't end that way. Certainly there are terrible traces of imperialism in our occupation of this land, but we can't let that defeat us.

Tarn: I'm with you there, very much so, but we have to get everyone to agree and this will take time. OK. I guess I was looking at another facet of the western lack of independence: looking to the Indian as father, to the European as father, to the easterner as father. The question of the weight of tradition. Well, this calls to mind another question. Bill, you are obviously a pillar of this evolving western ethos, while at the same time you are strongly involved in Catholicism, which is certainly not a majority religious situation in America. How do you see your Catholicism and your westernism as a nexus? Is there a connection, or is it just a historical accident in your particular situation?

Everson: It's an extremely problematic situation for me psychologically. I am archetypally tied into two distinct ideas. First, there is the American pragmatism which everyone here begins with, the Protestant ethic. Second, there is the Catholicism, which ties me to the history of Europe and Western civilization, its origins in Asia Minor. I made a break with my American pragmatism, and for eighteen and a half years lived in a monastery; then I reached a point where in a sense the American pragmatism caught up with me, after Vatican II, when the Church became social action oriented at the expense of mystical contemplation.

Bartlett: You left the Dominican order, not the Church.

Everson: Right, though I'm not in the sacraments. But I never left the Church. Once out of the monastery, I attempted to recover my aboriginal roots, to go back beyond the pragmatism and the Catholicism to a recovery of nature. I took the figure of the shaman as the most direct route to that. After all, I came to understand Catholicism through the medieval tradition of the vocation of the monk, and it seemed only natural that I might understand my aboriginal roots through the vocation of the shaman. The shaman is the most crystallized symbolic entity in this context, and so I began to shamanize—which, in a sense, as an artist I'd been doing all along. It was simply that now I could make a conscious attribution through animism back into the instinctual, which is the basis of the archetypal. Jung's theory of the archetypes is the method by which I can relate these three cultural levels. The project isn't complete, though, because I've not yet changed my life enough. But currently I'm writing my autobiographical epic as an attempt to bring these aspects together. Actually, I never realized that until this moment, but I see it clearly. In some way all three levels will come together there, which brings me back to the idea of transmutation. That is the function of the artist in society. Jeffers could stand aloof from whether or not the East Coast validated him, knowing that the future would. I have the same kind of faith that he did, but I can't bring myself to say the hell with you, that I'm putting my stakes on a thousand years from now. I just can't live that conviction of Jeffers's. I feel myself driven to heal the wound in the American psyche, the tension between the East and the West. And until the East validates the West the nation cannot be healed. I just can't let it go.

Bartlett: Which brings us back to the Pulitzer Prize.

Everson: It would go a long way to heal the rift. I agree with Nathaniel that the award itself is not all that distinguished actually, but as symbolic gesture it would mean acceptance.

Tarn: Well, what you've just said is very beautiful. I feel it may have some relation to my triad of "vocal," "silence," and "choral." It helps me see how with a certain view of the archetype you might transcend various political realities which seem to run directly counter to it. But after all, I continue to feel that an *American Indian poet* might still question your right or my right to that view. This seems in some ways to raise that spectre of violence again.

Bartlett: And yet most Indian poets, like Wendy Rose and Simon Ortiz, write in English.

Tarn: That's something history has forced them into.

Bartlett: Of course. But history has forced Bill into his position also. Leslie Silko makes many good points about cultural imperialism, but it's interesting that Bill and Snyder have come to their positions very consciously, while many Indian writers might well dismiss the question of their language by saying simply that history has forced them into it. Which is not a satisfactory answer to a very complex problem. After all, Indian writers who write in English, it might be argued, perpetuate cultural imperialism through their art. That the true Indian artists are those people who stay in the pueblos close to their root languages and traditions, though of course it is more complex than that. But back to what you were asking Bill, Nathaniel, your case is very similar—Judaism combined with your interest in Buddhism.

Tarn: In my case, I think it may well be irreconcilable. Bill has found a coherent way of bringing his contradictions together. But I remain in contradictions which sometimes cease to be beautiful. My own situation sometimes causes me abject despair simply because there are so many strands. I've come to believe that the artistic, political, and sociological situation in our time has become so complex that the only thing the artist can do is remain in a state of contradiction and give voice(s) to it, at least until history brings about a transmutation. But the artist is not in the position to effect this: she/he is not history. I have a very high view of Bill's faith in this matter, but in reality I think that, as you say, he can only do this in his head. Unfortunately, your head is not the world out there. I could go into detail on the relation between my Judaism and my Buddhism, but that would lead to autobiography, which isn't really the point of this.

Bartlett: But obviously, without the vision in your head you can't effect it in the world.

Tarn: Sure, and it's that vision, I suppose, which may break us out of the international East/West axis in favor of a more circular view. It got us into space, for example, though what bothers me there is the tremendous deadness of the place. Don't you hanker sometimes for another planet out there, functioning instead of being just a dead mass? I suppose we have to push on further.

Everson: Through astrology I know they are not dead masses, they are functioning. It's my link to the dimension we were speaking about before; purely symbolic, but there it is.

Tarn: Well, that's another of your beautiful notions that I'm not so sure about. Geez, I feel like a party-pooper!

Bartlett: Is your sense of this functioning as something abstracted from human consciousness?

Everson: No. In terms of it. The archetype relates to the instincts, but it is also operating out there. There is always a dichotomy between the subjective and the objective, two beads on the same string. The planet activates a potentiality within us. If it weren't doing it, we wouldn't recognize it at all. There is much out there that we don't recognize because it is not activating any potentiality within the race. When that material comes it will work through the symbolic mode so that we will recognize it. The result is that the symbolic is therefore superior to all other truth. Hard for the scientist to accept.

Tarn: I guess I may have more trouble with the way this material is usually handled than with the material itself. Most "New Age" handling seems to me to be the tail end of the weakest side of the "counter culture." It is sentimental, anti-intellectual, gushy, and wretchedly apolitical in every sense.

Bartlett: Yet look at something as simple as biorhythms, which you see at work in athletes all the time. Some days John McEnroe doesn't give up a point, a whole basketball team shoots 70 percent, or one can touch Marcus Allen—then other days it all falls apart. Some days we are so in tune with our bodies that it's beyond understanding, wonderfully transcendent; other times the timing or whatever is all off. It seems to me that this shift is not simply psychological, but rather muscular. Now if this is true, the rhythm might as well connect with the planets as anything else.

Tarn: You've got a point, and I don't want to deny that, though I don't think "might as well" is very conclusive. It's just that some of the same problems I have with the archetypal theory come into play here. But I'd like to turn to one final point. Again, reading *Birth of a Poet* I came across the following: "Americans cannot create a clerkly caste, not even by joining the university." But isn't that exactly what happened in America? By joining universities haven't poets created a clerkly caste, especially through the artificial production of writers by the MFA machine? All these babies who've done most of their living in test tubes?

Bartlett: I think Bill was alluding there to Auden's notion that the British writer traditionally thinks of himself as a member of a clerkly caste, while the American writer thinks of himself as an aristocracy of one.

Tarn: Not *all* British writers, surely. Auden was class-bound? But *are* the writing schools a question of an aristocracy of one?

Everson: No, which is exactly why I said that.

Tarn: I see. So you would argue that while it appears to be happening, in fact it's not successful. It's not going to produce the great voice.

Everson: But on the other hand, Thomas Wolfe went through the whole system, yet he's considered to be almost the archetypal poet. Certainly nobody would mistake him for an academic, yet Faulkner thought of him as the greatest American novelist.

Bartlett: And he's not often taught in the universities.

Tarn: I didn't know Faulkner felt that way.

Everson: In an interview someone asked him to rate American writers. He said Wolfe was first, he himself second, Hemingway third. Someone quoted that to John Berryman in his *Paris Review* interview and he almost fainted. I guess that points to the difference between Berryman and Faulkner. Wolfe was the greatest celebrator we've seen of the American earth.

Bartlett: But the lack of critical attention takes us back to the question of how much is there to say in a classroom (or in an article) about the great indigenous American writers like Whitman and Wolfe. Emerson, Jeffers, Ginsberg. I gave a paper at U. C. Davis on the Language poets a few days ago, and the first question to be asked was, "This is all fine, but how do you *teach* one of these poems in an introductory literature class?" As if poems were being written to be taught. Obviously, you can say much more in a critical sense—especially if you are drawn to poststructuralism or deconstruction or whatever—about a poem by Stevens than by, say, Williams. And Stevens's sensibility is thoroughly European.

Tarn: Yes, I must admit that I often find it hard to read Stevens as an American poet. On the other hand, the hell with exclusions!

Bartlett: And we don't want to fall into a kind of simplistic McCarthyism—who is the more "American." Yet the question of canon in late-twentieth-century America comes down to what and who is taught in the universities. And there it comes down to which poets and fiction writers can give you the most critical mileage, or mileage in the classroom. I just finished two full weeks on Ginsberg in a course I'm teaching, and I have to admit it was a trial. I was constantly reaching outside the work to fill the hour. Going outside is absolutely fine, and in fact to my mind is even preferable to the various New Critical fictions which still have hold on English departments.

Tarn: The expectation of exegesis. When the whole literary situation is keyed into the university as a canon-creating mechanism, those people who can be taught in class because of a certain complexity will be at the top of the canon. It's a self-perpetuating system. Though let's not forget that there are alternative canons being created all the time. I was looking at *Four Letters on the Archetype,* and what comes out there is the tremendous importance of Lawrence *as an American.* Here we get into the whole problem of the English over against the American canon. Today Lawrence has tremendous difficulty being accepted simply as a poet in England, and yet he is single-handedly the great alternative to that whole other traditional U.K. canon. When you look at his work you realize that he had made the passage. It's remarkable. But again, the British ghetto in the East conspires with the ghetto in Britain to keep Lawrence out of the whole system. The transmutation *has* taken place, but the god-damned East will not acknowledge it.

Bartlett: I don't have your faith in alternative canons, however. Most people, especially adolescents, simply don't read, and if the few university students who do are left in the hands of a few academics who have a very narrow view of what poetry is and should be, then a whole body of work is going to disappear. Publishers won't, or can't, do much about it. Even James Laughlin says that if you don't make it with the "professors" you're as good as dead. The American reading public doesn't keep poetry in print, classes of twenty students do.

Tarn: If this is true, even if the great voice arises there may be no one to listen to it.

Bartlett: And the further complexity here is that as much as we rail against the tunnel vision of universities, they rescued Emily Dickinson and Herman Melville. The reading public could not have cared less.

Everson: I began as an antiacademic, but no more. After all, I taught in the university for ten years.

Bartlett: And Kenneth Rexroth did the same.

Everson: As a poet I know I live by it. I agree that there is little poetry read outside it. I know that if I don't make it in the university I will not survive. But I know I will make it there. And I'll make it in America. There we go again—pure faith.

Tarn: Faith against the dragon of sociology.

Notes

Chapter One

1. Eliot Weinberger, "At the Death of Kenneth Rexroth," *Works on Paper* (New York: New Directions, 1986), 111–19.

2. D. H. Lawrence, *Selected Poems,* edited by Kenneth Rexroth (New York: New Directions, 1948), 18–19.

3. Leslie Fiedler, "Some Uses and Failures of Feeling," *Partisan Review,* vol. 15, no. 8 (August 1948):924–31.

4. Kenneth Rexroth, "Ids and Animuses," *New York Times Book Review* (March 17, 1968):4.

5. Kenneth Rexroth, "The Function of Poetry and the Place of the Poet in Society," *World Outside the Window: Selected Essays,* edited by Bradford Morrow (New York: New Directions, 1987), 1–7.

6. Kenneth Rexroth, *The Collected Longer Poems* (New York: New Directions, 1968), vii–ix.

7. Lawrence Lipton, "Notes Toward an Understanding of Kenneth Rexroth with Special Attention to 'The Homestead Called Damascus,'" *Quarterly Review of Literature,* vol. 9, no. 2 (1957):37–46.

8. Morgan Gibson, *Kenneth Rexroth* (Boston: Twayne, 1972).

9. Kenneth Rexroth, *The Signature of All Things* (New York: New Directions, 1950), 3.

10. David Perkins, *A History of Modern Poetry: Modernism and After* (Cambridge: Harvard University Press, 1987), 25.

Chapter Two

1. See on Olson Charles Boer's "Poetry and Psyche" and Jed Rasula's "Charles Olson and Robert Duncan: A muthologistical Grounding" in *Spring 1979;* Robert Bly, *Leaping Poetry* (Boston: Beacon Press, 1975) and *News of the Universe* (San Francisco: Sierra Club Books, 1980); Clayton Eshleman, *Hades in Manganese* (Santa Barbara: Black Sparrow Press, 1981).

2. See especially Jung's 1934 interview, "Does the World Stand on the Verge of a Spiritual Rebirth?" in *C. G. Jung Speaking,* ed. by William McGuire and R. F. C. Hull (Princeton: Princeton University Press, 1977), 67–75.

3. Everson, "From the Depths of a Void," in *Earth Poetry: Selected Essays and Interviews* (Berkeley: Oyez, 1980), 75.

4. "Dionysus and the Beat Generation," *Ibid.,* 21–28.

5. From the manuscript of Everson's introduction to the reissue of White's *God and the Unconscious,* forthcoming from Spring Publications.

6. Victor White, *God and the Unconscious* (Cleveland: World Publishing Company, 1952), 67, 78.

7. *Ibid.,* 126.

8. Information on shamanism in the following paragraphs is drawn from Everson's source, Andreas Lommel, *Shamanism: The Beginnings of Art* (New York: McGraw-Hill, 1966).

9. Mircea Eliade, *Shamanism* (Princeton: Princeton University Press, 1964), 388.

10. *Earth Poetry,* 189.

11. Albert Gelpi, *The Tenth Muse* (Cambridge: Harvard University Press, 1975), 45–46.

12. C. G. Jung, "On the Relation of Analytical Pscychology to Poetic Art," in *Contributions to Analytical Psychology.*

13. "On Psychical Energy," *ibid.*, 56.

14. *Ibid.*, 53.

15. C. G. Jung, *Psychological Types* (London, 1953), 616.

16. Jung, *Symbols of Transformation* (Princeton: Princeton University Press, 1956), 157.

17. *Psychological Types*, 467.

18. See Chapter 10, "General Descriptions of the Types," *ibid.*, for further treatment.

19. Morris Philipson, *Outline of Jungian Aesthetics* (Evanston: Northwestern University Press, 1963), 104–5.

20. *Ibid.*

21. C. G. Jung, *Aion* (Princeton: Princeton University Press, 1968), 11–22.

22. C. G. Jung, *Mysterium Conjunctionis* (Princeton: Princeton University Press, 1963), 409.

23. Gelpi, *Tenth Muse*, 208.

24. Albert Gelpi, "Everson/Antoninus: Contending with the Shadow," an afterword to Everson's *Veritable Years* (Santa Barbara: Black Sparrow Press, 1978), 361.

25. C. G. Jung, *Symbols of Transformation* (Princeton: Princeton University Press, 1956), 269.

26. *Ibid.*

27. C. G. Jung, *The Psychology of the Transference* (Princeton: Princeton University Press, 1969), 146.

28. *Aion*, 205.

29. See June Singer, *Androgyny* (New York: Anchor Press, 1976), 125–50.

Chapter Four

1. See brief discussions of the poem in Bob Steuding, *Gary Snyder* (Boston: Twayne, 1976), and Bert Almon, *Gary Snyder* (Boise: Boise State University Western Writers Series, no. 37, 1979). The most useful item on *Myths & Texts* thus far is Howard McCord's short pamphlet "Some Notes on Gary Sny-

der's *Myths & Texts*" (Berkeley: Sand Dollar, 1971), which attempts to identify many of the allusions and quotations in the poem.

2. *Myths & Texts* was first published by Totem Press in association with Corinth Books in 1960. The volume went through a number of printings, though as often as not was out of print, especially through the early seventies. In 1978, New Directions finally brought out an edition of the book, with a new preface by Snyder.

3. Joseph Campbell, *The Hero with a Thousand Faces* (Princeton: Princeton University Press, 1949). According to Campbell, "The standard path of the mythological adventure of the hero is a magnification of the formula represented in the rites of passage: separation—initiation—return: which might be named the nuclear unit of the monomyth [the word is taken from Joyce's *Finnegans Wake*]. A hero ventures forth from the world of common day into a region of supernatural wonder; fabulous forces are there encountered and a decisive victory is won; the hero comes back from this mysterious adventure with the power to bestow boons on his fellow man" (30). Steuding notes Campbell's influences on the structure of *M&T* in his study.

4. I am grateful to McCord's "Notes" for some of the identifications included here.

5. Snyder's own note in McCord (note 22).

6. Campbell, 193.

7. McCord, note 42.

8. Quoted in Campbell, 374.

Chapter Six

1. Nathaniel Tarn, "Child as Father to Man in the American Uni-verse," *American Poetry* (Winter 1984) 1,2:67.

2. Doris Sommer. "America as Desire(d): Nathaniel Tarn's Poetry of the Outsider as Insider," *American Poetry* (Fall 1984) 2,1:13–35.

3. Thom Gunn, *The Occasions of Poetry* (London, Faber & Faber, 1982), 175.

4. Lee Bartlett, ed., *Talking Poetry: Conversations in the Workshop* (Albuquerque, University of New Mexico Press, 1987), 99.

5. Gunn, *Occasions,* 176.

6. *Ibid.,* 119.

7. *Ibid.,* 134.

8. Bartlett, *Talking Poetry,* 89–90.

9. Gunn, *Occasions,* 173.

10. See Alan Bold, *Thom Gunn and Ted Hughes* (Edinburgh: Oliver & Boyd, 1976).

11. Gregory Woods, *Articulate Flesh: Male Homo-eroticism & Modern Poetry* (New Haven: Yale University Press, 1987), 212–30.

12. Bartlett, *Talking Poetry,* 100.

13. Bold, *Gunn and Hughes,* 25.

14. *Ibid.,* 31.

15. Gunn, *Occasions,* 181–82.

16. Bartlett, *Talking Poetry,* 97.

17. W. H. Auden, ed., *The Criterion Book of Modern American Verse* (New York: Criterion Books, 1956), 17–18.

18. Bartlett, *Talking Poetry,* 99.

19. Gunn, *Occasions,* 182.

20. Bartlett, *Talking Poetry,* 91.

21. Tarn, "Uni-verse," 71.

22. Lee Bartlett, *Nathaniel Tarn: A Descriptive Bibliography* (Jefferson: McFarland, 1987), 26.

23. Tarn, "Uni-verse," 72–73.

24. Bartlett, *Tarn,* 36.

25. Tarn, "Uni-verse," 73.

26. Bartlett, *Talking Poetry,* 211.

27. Tarn, "Uni-verse," 74–75.

Bibliography

Allen, Donald, and Warren Tallman, eds. *The Poetics of the New American Poetry*. New York: Grove Press, 1973.

Altieri, Charles. *Enlarging the Temple: New Directions in American Poetry During the 1960s*. Lewisberg, Pa.: Bucknell University Press, 1979.

Andrews, Bruce, and Charles Bernstein, eds. *The L=A=N=G=U=A=G=E Book*. Carbondale: Southern Illinois University Press, 1984.

Barthes, Roland. *Elements of Semiology*. London: Jonathan Cape, 1967.

———. *Writing Degree Zero*. London: Jonathan Cape, 1967.

Bartlett, Lee. *Talking Poetry: Conversations in the Workshop With Contemporary Poets*. Albuquerque: University of New Mexico Press, 1987.

———. *William Everson: The Life of Brother Antoninus*. New York: New Directions, 1988.

Belitt, Ben. *Adam's Dream: A Preface to Translation*. New York: Grove Press, 1978.

Bernstein, Charles. *Content's Dream: Essays 1975–1984*. Los Angeles: Sun & Moon Press, 1986.

Bold, Alan. *Thom Gunn and Ted Hughes*. Edinburgh: Oliver & Boyd, 1976.

Burroughs, William. *The Adding Machine: Selected Essays.* New York: Seaver Books, 1986.

Cage, John. *Silence: Lectures and Writings.* Cambridge, Mass.: M.I.T. Press, 1966.

Campbell, Joseph. *The Hero with a Thousand Faces.* Princeton: Princeton University Press, 1949.

Charters, Ann. *The Beats: Literary Bohemians in Postwar America* (2 vols.). Detroit: Gale, 1983.

Coolidge, Clark. *Solution Passage: Poems 1978–1981.* Los Angeles: Sun & Moon Press, 1986.

Derrida, Jacques. *Writing and Difference.* Chicago: University of Chicago Press, 1978.

———. *Speech and Phenomena.* Evanston: Northeastern University Press, 1973.

Duberman, Martin. *Black Mountain: An Exploration in Community.* New York: Dutton, 1972.

Duncan, Robert. *Bending the Bow.* New York: New Directions, 1968.

———. *Derivations: Selected Poems, 1950–1956.* London: Fulcrum Press, 1968.

———. *Fictive Certainties.* New York: New Directions, 1985.

———. *Ground Work: Before the War.* New York: New Directions, 1984.

———. *Ground Work: In the Dark.* New York: New Directions, 1987.

———. *The Opening of the Field.* New York: Grove Press, 1960.

———. *Roots and Branches.* New York: Charles Scribners' Sons, 1964.

Eliade, Mircea. *Shamanism: Archaic Techniques of Ecstasy.* Princeton: Princeton University Press, 1964.

———. *Patanjali and Yoga.* New York: Funk & Wagnalls, 1969.

———. *Yoga: Immortality and Freedom.* Princeton: Princeton University Press, 1958.

Everson, William. *Archetype West: The Pacific Coast as a Literary Region.* Berkeley: Oyez, 1976.

———. *Birth of a Poet.* Lee Bartlett, ed. Santa Barbara: Black Sparrow Press, 1982.

———. *Earth Poetry: Selected Essays and Interviews.* Lee Bartlett, ed. Berkeley: Oyez, 1980.

———. *The Residual Years.* New York: New Directions, 1968.

———. *The Veritable Years.* Santa Barbara: Black Sparrow Press, 1978.

Faas, Ekbert, ed. *Towards a New American Poetics.* Santa Barbara: Black Sparrow Press, 1978.

———. *Young Robert Duncan: Portrait of the Poet as Homosexual in Society.* Santa Barbara: Black Sparrow Press, 1983.

Ferlinghetti, Lawrence, and Nancy J. Peters. *Literary San Francisco.* San Francisco: City Lights / Harper & Row, 1980.

Fredman, Stephen. *Poet's Prose: The Crisis in American Verse.* Cambridge: Cambridge University Press, 1983.

Gefin, Laszlo K. *Ideogram: History of a Poetic Method.* Austin: University of Texas Press, 1982.

Gelpi, Albert. *A Coherent Splendor: The American Poetic Renaissance, 1910–1950.* Cambridge: Cambridge University Press, 1987.

———. *The Tenth Muse: The Psyche of the American Poet.* Cambridge, Mass.: Harvard University Press, 1975.

Gibson, Morgan. *Kenneth Rexroth.* Boston: Twayne, 1972.

Ginsberg, Allen. *Allen Verbatim: Lectures on Poetry, Politics, Consciousness.* Edited by Gordon Ball. New York: McGraw-Hill, 1974.

Gunn, Thom. *Moly.* London: Faber and Faber, 1971.

———. *The Occasions of Poetry: Essays in Criticism and Autobiography.* Edited by Clive Wilmer. London: Faber and Faber, 1982.

———. *The Passages of Joy.* London: Faber and Faber, 1982.

———. *Poems: 1950–1966.* London: Faber and Faber, 1969.

Honig, Edwin. *The Poet's Other Voice: Conversations in Literary Translation.* Amherst: University of Massachusetts Press, 1985.

Jung, C. G. *C. G. Jung Speaking: Interviews and Encounters.* Princeton: Princeton University Press, 1977.

————. *The Collected Works* (19 volumes). Princeton: Princeton University Press, 1953–79.

Knight, Arthur, and Kit Knight. *Beat Angels.* California, Pa.: the unspeakable visions of the individual, 1982.

————. *The Beat Journey.* California, Pa.: the unspeakable visions of the individual, 1978.

Leary, Timothy. *Flashbacks: An Autobiography.* Los Angeles: J. P. Tarcher, 1983.

Lommel, Andreas. *Shamanism: The Beginnings of Art.* New York: McGraw-Hill, 1966.

Macksey, Richard, and Eugenio Donato. *The Structuralist Controversy.* Baltimore: Johns Hopkins University Press, 1972.

McClure, Michael. *The Beard.* Berkeley: Oyez, 1965.

————. *Ghost Tantras.* San Francisco: privately printed, 1964.

————. *Hymns to St. Geryon and Other Poems.* San Francisco: Auerhahn Press, 1959.

————. *Meat Science Essays.* San Francisco: City Lights, 1963; expanded edition, 1966.

————. *Passage.* Big Sur: Jonathan Williams, 1956.

————. *Scratching the Beat Surface.* San Francisco: North Point Press, 1982.

————. *Selected Poems.* New York: New Directions, 1986.

————. *September Blackberries.* New York: New Directions, 1974.

McCord, Howard. *Some Notes on Gary Snyder's Myths & Texts.* Berkeley: Sand Dollar, 1971.

McCoy, Alfred W. *The Politics of Heroin in Southeast Asia.* New York: Harper & Row, 1972.

Meltzer, David. *The San Francisco Poets.* New York: Ballantine, 1971.

Merleau-Ponty, Maurice. *Phenomenology of Perception.* London: Routledge & Kegan Paul, 1962.

Messerli, Douglas, ed. *"Language" Poetries: An Anthology.* New York: New Directions, 1987.

Norris, Christopher. *Derrida.* Cambridge, Mass.: Harvard University Press, 1987.

Olson, Charles. *Selected Writings.* Edited by Robert Creeley. New York: New Directions, 1966.

Palmer, Michael. *Blake's Newton.* Los Angeles: Black Sparrow Press, 1972.

———. *Circular Gates.* Los Angeles: Black Sparrow Press, 1974.

———. *Code of Signals: Recent Writings in Poetics.* Richmond: North Atlantic Books, 1983.

———. *First Figure.* San Francisco: North Point Press, 1984.

———. *Notes for Echo Lake.* San Francisco: North Point Press, 1981.

Parkinson, Thomas. *Poets, Poems, Movements.* Ann Arbor: UMI Research Press, 1987.

Perelman, Bob, ed. *Writing/Talks.* Carbondale: Southern Illinois University Press, 1985.

Perkins, David. *A History of Modern Poetry: Modernism and After.* Cambridge, Mass: Harvard University Press, 1987.

Perloff, Marjorie. *The Dance of the Intellect: Studies in the Poetry of the Pound Tradition.* Cambridge: Cambridge University Press, 1985.

———. *The Poetics of Indeterminacy.* Princeton: Princeton University Press, 1981.

Philipson, Morris. *Outline of a Jungian Aesthetics.* Evanston: Northwestern University Press, 1963.

Rexroth, Kenneth. *American Poetry in the Twentieth Century.* New York: Herder, 1971.

———. *The Collected Longer Poems.* New York: New Directions, 1968.

———. *The Collected Shorter Poems.* New York: New Directions, 1966.

————. *One Hundred Poems from the Chinese*. New York: New Directions, 1971.

————. *World Outside the Window: The Selected Essays*. Edited by Bradford Morrow. New York: New Directions, 1987.

Silliman, Ron. *In the American Tree*. Orono: National Poetry Foundation, 1986.

————. *The New Sentence*. New York: Roof Books, 1987.

Snyder, Gary. *Earth House Hold: Technical Notes & Queries to Fellow Dharma Revolutionaries*. New York: New Directions, 1969.

————. *Myths & Texts*. New York: Totem Press, 1960.

————. *The Old Ways*. San Francisco: City Lights Books, 1977.

————. *The Real Work: Interviews & Talks, 1964–1979*. Edited by William Scott McLean. New York: New Directions, 1980.

————. *Riprap & Cold Mountain Poems*. San Francisco: Four Seasons Foundation, 1965.

Steiner, Peter. *Russian Formalism: A Metapoetics*. Ithaca: Cornell University Press, 1984.

Tarn, Nathaniel. *At the Western Gates*. Santa Fe: Tooth of Time, 1985.

————. *Atitlan / Alashka: New and Selected Poems* (with Janet Rodney). Boulder: Brillig Works Press, 1979.

————. *The Beautiful Contradictions*. London: Cape Goliard Press, 1969.

————. *The Desert Mothers*. Grenada: Salt-Works Press, 1984.

————. *Lyrics for the Bride of God*. New York: New Directions, 1975.

————. *Old Savage / Young City*. London: Cape, 1964.

Vincent, Stephen, and Ellen Zweig, eds. *The Poetry Reading*. San Francisco: Momo's Press, 1981.

Wasson, R. Gordon. *Soma: Divine Mushroom of Immortality*. New York: Harcourt Brace Jovanovich, 1973.

Waley, Arthur. *Madly Singing in the Mountains*. Edited by Ivan Morris. New York: Walker and Company, 1970.

Watten, Barrett. *Total Syntax*. Carbondale: Southern Illinois University Press, 1985.

Weinberger, Eliot. *Works on Paper*. New York: New Directions, 1986.

Welch, Lew. *I Remain: The Letters of Lew Welch & The Correspondence of His Friends* (2 vols.). Edited by Donald Allen. Bolinas, Ca.: Grey Fox Press, 1980.

White, Victor. *God and the Unconscious*. Cleveland: World, 1952.

Whitehead, Alfred North. *Concept of Nature*. Cambridge: Cambridge University Press, 1920.

————. *Modes of Thought*. New York: Macmillan, 1938.

Wittgenstein, Ludwig. *The Blue and Brown Books*. London: Basil Blackwell, 1958.

————. *Philosophical Investigations*. London: Basil Blackwell & Mott, Ltd., 1958.

————. *Tractatus Logico-Philosophicus*. London: Routledge & Kegan Paul, 1961.

Woods, Gregory. *Articulate Flesh: Male Homo-Eroticism and Modern Poetry*. New Haven: Yale University Press, 1987.